HELPING PARENTS
WHO ABUSE
THEIR CHILDREN

HELPING PARENTS
WHO ABUSE
THEIR CHILDREN

A Comprehensive Approach for Intervention

By

SHARON R. PALLONE, B.S., L.H.D.

Founder and Executive Director
SCAN Volunteer Service, Inc.
Little Rock, Arkansas

and

LOIS C. MALKEMES, R.N., Ph.D.

Chairperson, Board of Directors
SCAN Volunteer Service, Inc.
Little Rock, Arkansas

With a Foreword by

Ray E. Helfer, M.D.

Department of Human Development
Michigan State University
East Lansing, Michigan

CHARLES C THOMAS • PUBLISHER
Springfield • Illinois • U.S.A.

Published and Distributed Throughout the World by

CHARLES C THOMAS • PUBLISHER
2600 South First Street
Springfield, Illinois 62717

© *1984 by* CHARLES C THOMAS • PUBLISHER

ISBN 0-398-05032-5

Library of Congress Catalog Card Number: 84-2697

With THOMAS BOOKS *careful attention is given to all details of manufacturing and
design. It is the Publisher's desire to present books that are satisfactory as to their physical
qualities and artistic possibilities and appropriate for their particular use.* THOMAS
BOOKS *will be true to those laws of quality that assure a good name and good will.*

Printed in the United States of America
Q-R-3

Library of Congress Cataloging in Publication Data

Pallone, Sharon R.
  Helping parents who abuse their children.

  Bibliography: p.
  Includes index.
  1. Child abuse — Services — United States. 2. Child
abuse — United States Prevention. 3. Family social
work — United States. I. Malkemes, Lois C. II. Title.
HV741.P335 1984   362.7'044   84-2697
ISBN 0-398-05032-5

This book is dedicated to abused children and parents with a child abuse problem, who are now contributing adults.

Also, we dedicate this book to Jolly K., who gave us support, information, and recognition.

FOREWORD

ANY child who experiences or witnesses child abuse, neglect, sexual exploitation or spouse abuse throughout his/her childhood is learning a bizzare form of interpersonal interactions, especially between those who like each other. The bottom line for these children is extremely limited skills in developing and maintaining close personal relationships. They have learned little during their childhood of how to treat nicely those they like the most. In the jargon of the professional, these children enter adulthood poorly socialized.

The process of resocializing those whose skills are so limited is slow, and often painful. Like swimming, it surely is easier to learn as a kid. But, many who haven't had that good fortune can improve greatly with help. The need is major, for millions of young adults have experienced most unusual rearing practices while they were growing up.

From this need emerged SCAN Volunteers, Inc. A group of dedicated professionals and volunteers who are effectively working to help retrain those who were reared in the abusive environment and are now trying to "shake loose" its tentacles and rear their children differently.

A variety of programs has been established to utilize the peer helper as a retrainer. Parent aides and lay therapists are most commonly referred to in the literature. SCAN Volunteers, Inc. has led the way in this endeavor, especially with the organizational abilities, training program, extension beyond county lines, and the development of a curriculum. Their success is a result of these vital components plus highly motivated, well trained and persistent volunteers.

No volunteer program can be effective without well trained professionals to supervise. SCAN Volunteers realized this from the outset.

The importance of this book lies in its goal to extend this experience to others, thereby expanding the program even further. One of the biggest problems facing those who work in the field of child abuse is the difficulty one confronts in trying to disseminate good ideas. Pallone's and Malkemes's book will help overcome this barrier. Many more young adults who need the help of the SCAN Volunteer will benefit.

Ray E. Helfer, M.D.

PREFACE

CHILD abuse is receiving increased attention as a major family, community, and national problem. Most of the literature focuses on issues relating to definitions, causes, and roles of various professional groups in identifying, investigating, and coordination strategies for dealing with child abuse. Little attention is given to what family interventions are successful and how to implement them. Attention is given to treatment or intervention strategies primarily from a psychological and professional therapy prospective.

In this book we provide a how-to and hands-on approach for an individual, staff person, or volunteer involved in working with families with a child abuse problem. We combine an integrative theoretical approach that views child abuse as a multi-dimensional, multi-causal problem that must be dealt with within the context of the families' broad social environment, that is, the neighborhood, place of employment, community and culture.

In the following pages we bring the reader from *A New Beginning* to the way that new beginning is accomplished in *Putting Theory Into Action*. We end by discussing the structure of the SCAN program that supports the therapeutic approach in *SCAN Volunteer Service, Inc.*

Unfortunately, while we know much about families with a child abuse problem, there is no single approach that provides the magic answer to the successful elimination of abuse within all families. This book suggests an approach that is successful for a great number of children and their families. It can easily be adapted for implementation in your state and program. We invite you to adapt these suggested strategies in your work with families who have a child abuse problem.

Throughout the book we have used the pronoun he/she interchangeably.

ACKNOWLEDGMENTS

WE extend our appreciation to the entire SCAN staff and Board of Directors, whose endless efforts have made a difference in homes where child abuse once was the norm, to state and community agencies, whose support and acceptance of the intervention model made it possible for SCAN to grow and flourish; to the Arkansas General Assembly, whose financial and emotional support has given us longevity; to the National Exchange Club Foundation for the Prevention of Child Abuse and Neglect and the National Council of Juvenile and Family Court Judges, for giving us the opportunity to expand this theoretical model to other states; to Berkeley Planning Associates and the National Institute of Mental Health, Research Division, for their evaluation of SCAN, Inc.; to C. Henry Kempe, M.D. and Ray Helfer, M.D. for their early writings and research in the field; and to all others who found SCAN important to include in their research.

In addition several people were invaluable to the development of SCAN and the writing of this book: Lloyd Young, M.D., who had a vision for treatment of families with a child abuse problem; Ardelia Womack, who helped us penetrate the bureacracy; Rosalie Anderson, who provided the impetus for us to record the theoretical treatment model; Jackie Waddle, whose writing at the end of this book captures the essence of the relationship between lay therapist and parents with a child abuse problem; Eleanor Mille, Fran Millard, and Mike Vogler, whose energies were critical to the completion of the manuscript; Taibi Kahler, Ph.D., whose thinking gave us guidance; and to Daphnia Smith, who typed the chaotic manuscript into an orderly book.

We thank our families and many friends for their support during the long arduous task of developing SCAN and during the writing of this manuscript. We are indebted to our families for teaching us how to parent. A special appreciation to Pete and Mike Pallone, who continued to grow and develop over the past eleven years during the development of SCAN.

We further acknowledge that this publication was made possible, in part, by Grant No. 90-CO-1979 from the U.S. Children's Bureau, Administration for Children, Youth and Families, Office of Human Development Services, Department of Health and Human Services.

CONTENTS

HELPING PARENTS
WHO ABUSE
THEIR CHILDREN

Chapter 1

A NEW BEGINNING

MURPHY CASE STUDY

WE remember when we first met the Murphy family. They were referred by juvenile court because a neighbor called saying that she heard loud cries of children in the mobile home next door. Upon arrival, we found a young mother holding her infant, with a four-year-old standing beside her. Both of the children had bruises and appeared to be extremely withdrawn. Mrs. Murphy refused to talk with us but agreed to come with her husband to Parents Anonymous that night. When they came to the meeting they were extremely hostile, belligerent, and possessive of the children.

During the meeting, Mr. Murphy related that he ran away from home at the age of eight and that since he had survived this long he did not need anyone's help. Mrs. Murphy agreed that any attempt to help her family was ridiculous. She shared that her home life had been filled with abuse and that she had left home at fifteen. She stated that her two sisters had probably been abused in some institution. She remembered that her maternal grandmother had severely abused her mother, which included physical abuse, deprivation of food and clothes, and sadistic emotional abuse. Her parents' marriage had been violent, but her mother stayed with her father because she did not know how to provide for herself.

During the meeting, the children sat perfectly still, watching both parents intently. They seemed to be ready to antici-

3

pate and prevent an aggressive move toward them. Finally, the baby was placed on the floor. When he attempted to crawl, he fell to one side. As soon as the meeting was over, we persuaded the parents to take the children to the hospital for an examination, including long bone x-rays. Jimmy, the infant, had sustained old fractures that were healing. He was given a diagnosis of failure to thrive. Melissa, the four-year-old, revealed old and new bruising. A court hearing was arranged, and the children were placed in foster care.

We spent most of the following days listening to Mr. Murphy's outbursts of anger and resentment toward authority. They wanted our help in order to have the children returned, but they continued to resist any invitation to change their behavior.

We were successful in assisting Mr. Murphy in getting a different job. We spent a great deal of time explaining the legal and social service systems, and we frequently discussed why parents cannot treat their children as possessions. Mrs. Murphy wanted to see a psychologist, and Mr. Murphy seemed resigned to her having therapy. Both of them agreed to continue in Parents Anonymous and work with us. Mr. Murphy began to call us for advice and help. He seemed more willing to trust and began to believe that we would not lie to him or betray him.

After several months, Mr. Murphy reluctantly agreed to join his wife in therapy. Both talked about their childhood and earlier marriages and the problems they thought influenced their feelings for the children. Mrs. Murphy stated that she loved her children, but she realized that they had experienced a difficult time. Slowly, they both decided they wanted to make changes and become better parents. We observed that their self-esteem and independence seemed to be increasing. They were less isolated and more willing to participate openly in Parents Anonymous meetings.

Their visits with the children were more relaxed and both parents showed more positive interaction. Both stated that the children feared them and that they would need time to show the children their love. Mrs. Murphy hoped that Melissa had known she loved her even when she hurt her. Both children began to show affection toward the parents and the parents acted more tolerant and patient. They seemed to understand that only they could make the necessary changes in their behavior to get the children back.

RICE CASE STUDY

Barbara and Jack Rice were referred at the time of the death of their twenty-month-old son, Wayne, who weighed twelve pounds. The cause of death was noted as malnutrition and dehydration. The initial interview with the family revealed some very classic child abuse dynamics.

Barbara stated that she was a perfectionist. She was extremely concerned about her situation and could not believe that she killed Wayne. Jack was agreeable to the interview and freely gave support to his wife. Barbara talked openly about her life. She had lived with her aunt for a short period of time and then she was placed in foster care. She was moved frequently from foster home to foster home and remembered her decision not to feel love or attachment for anyone, believing that meaningful people would leave her. She stated that everyone loved babies, but she could not remember anyone loving her.

She married Jack and immediately became pregnant with Scott. She had wanted a boy and had felt excited about having a baby whom she could love. She explained Scott's weight of twenty-three pounds at five years of age by saying that he was an active child who never enjoyed eating. She continued by stating that her pregnancy with Wayne had been a miserable experience. She was sick most of the time and blamed him for her illness. She stated that when he was born he looked just like her and that he looked at her in an evil way. He could not do things that other babies could do and was always determined to get her.

When he was an infant, she had not wanted to hold him or feed him because he was mean and stubborn. However, she soon felt scared and, because he was so thin, took him to the hospital. The physician told her that if she did not feed him properly, they would have to take the child away. She felt more fear and refused to go back to any hospital. She attempted to feed him inappropriate foods, such as canned beans and regular meat. He refused to eat.

Barbara did not have friends, stating that she felt very alone. She changed jobs frequently because she felt inadequate and thought that people did not think she did a good job.

We continued to work with Barbara and Jack, with the initial intervention designed to help Barbara with legal assistance and counsel. She had been indicted for murder. We worked with her intensely while she awaited trial, and we were able to provide Barbara with the mothering she had missed. Barbara participated in activities with our families and stated that she had been adopted.

Barbara went to trial, was convicted of murder, and was sent to prison. We continued to spend time with her while she carried out her sentence. The prison officials agreed for Barbara to visit with her son, who had been placed in foster care, and we were able to arrange for the visits. When Barbara was released, she continued the schooling that she had started in prison. She was soon employed at a job that she maintained. We gave Barbara information about child development, while arranging for visits with her son. It was necessary for Scott to be seen at a child guidance center. A counselor worked with Barbara and Scott together and stated that she had made tremendous progress toward understanding her responsibility to the people around her. She learned how to nurture, as well as accept nurturance. It was obvious that her self-concept was changing.

Barbara became pregnant for the third time and seemed content with the idea of having a boy or a girl. She was developing friendships with other families who had children and seemed to be watching their parenting skills. The pregnancy was uneventful. We arranged to be in the delivery room with Barbara and Jack when their baby girl, Ruth Ann, was born. Barbara held the newborn as a nurturing mother, and she was able to demonstrate great changes in her mothering ability. Scott was returned from foster care, when the baby was six months old.

Throughout the years of working with families with a child abuse problem, we maintain our original beliefs that parents who abuse their children, love their children. They can benefit from treatment, rather than prosecution. They can provide a safe home for their children and become positively functioning adults. The stereotype of parents who abuse their children is still one that envisions a middle-aged, mean, sadistic, hostile, unkept individual who cannot be helped. However, we have yet to meet this person, after working with hundreds of parents with a child abuse problem. The people we have met are young, scared, desperate for help, in need of hope, and longing for stability.

The two families with a child abuse problem that we present here show us the depth, scope, and tragedy of this national problem. With long-term intensive intervention, both of these dysfunctional parents are presently providing safe homes for their children and are contributing adults to society.

Chapter 2

CHARACTERISTICS OF ABUSIVE PARENTS

A REVIEW of the child abuse literature, research, and interviews with child protective services staff reveals a wide variety of characteristics of parents who abuse their children. Although the majority of these attributes are based upon clinical impressions by workers in the field, rather than upon research, numerous writers identify a common set of characteristics of abusive parents. The set of characteristics most often includes isolation, dependence, role reversal, low self-esteem, impulsiveness, overcontrol, a low tolerance for frustration, inadequate parenting, and unsuccessful or lack of positive social experiences. These are further explored in this chapter.

THEORETICAL FRAMEWORK

Understanding the dynamics of child abuse rests on the understanding of normal growth and development and the learning that occurs in that process. The goal of normal development is a healthy adult who has a positive self-concept, a sense of interdependence with his environment, and a maturity that provides for a sharing relationship with another adult, raising a family, and beginning the cycle again.

Erikson's developmental stages provide a framework for understanding the normal, and thus the abnormal developmental processes, that results in an understanding of the dynamics of child abuse.[1] Erikson suggests that satisfactory accomplishment of each stage is necessary for healthy development.

The first stage is the achievement of a basic sense of trust. The mother-child relationship is of great importance in this stage of development. When the relationship is well developed, the child is comfortable with feeding and having his needs met. This provides predictability, a feeling of inner comfort, and happiness.[2] It is when this relationship between mother and child is not well developed that feelings of uncertainty and a basic sense of mistrust occurs.

The second stage focuses on the development of a sense of autonomy.[3] It is during this stage that individuals begin to discover that their behaviors impact their environment in various ways. The individual begins to learn to evaluate his behaviors and their effects upon others with whom he interacts. It is this evaluation that leads to self-esteem. The dangers of not successfully completing this stage result in a minute self-control, a sense of sadness, and a negative self-concept.

Central to the third stage of development is the sense of initiative versus the sense of guilt. In this stage the child has more energy and more direction toward the desirable, which adds a dimension to autonomy.[4] The problem that can occur in this stage is the development of a sense of guilt about what the child wants to do. Because of his feelings of guilt, he acquiesces to parental demands. This individual feels scared, anxious, and sad. If these feelings are too controlled, they become rage and grief and the individual has the potential for turning against others.[5]

Acquiring a sense of industry is the fourth stage. This stage focuses on developing mastery over what the individual does. It is at this stage that the individual needs support and self-assurance as he attempts to become part of the larger society. Relationships with peers and adults take on a new importance in the development of a sense of worth and become important criteria to measure the individual's successes or failures.[6] When support, self-assurance and positive relations are not experienced, a sense of inferiority and inadequacy develop.[7]

The last stage of childhood development is that of developing a sense of identity.[8] It is during this stage that the individual becomes an interdependent member of society and begins to leave his dependency on the family. The importance of the movement from childhood to adulthood is emphasized by Erikson as a continuum of what persons have become during childhood and what they promise to become in the future. The major problematic outcome is role confusion.[9]

When an individual has not mastered the initial stages of child development satisfactorily, negative personality dynamics often result in child abuse. These characteristics help us understand parents with a child abuse problem and subsequently help in the development of programs.

ROLE REVERSAL DYNAMICS

For abusive parents, a number of underlying conflicts occur during Erikson's initial stages of a sense of mastery and sense of identity. Steele and Pollack, in their clinical study of abusive parents, observe the inability to parent,[10] unresolved identity conflicts, depression, and feelings of worthlessness, in addition to inadequate self-esteem.[11]

Any life crisis which reinforces the individual's low self-esteem leads to a desperate need for reassurance from his environment. However, because of the basic sense of mistrust that abusive parents have, they are unable to form effective relationships. Instead, parents who abuse their child turn to their child as a source of basic gratification for their needs.

Their extreme inadequacy, hopelessness, and despair about their inabilities to improve their lives damages the parent/child relationship and results in role reversal in which the parents demand support from the child, having assumed the dependent child role. This dynamic role can be evidenced in the parents' expression of unrealistic expectations for their child. As part of these unrealistic expectations, the parents project adult feelings and motives which are far beyond the child's cognitive developmental level. For example, the failure of a one-year-old child to control bladder functioning is seen as an expression of hate toward the parents. A three-year-old girl is severely punished for smiling at a stranger because the parents attribute this behavior as being seductive. The parents fear their child will grow up to be as awful as themselves, so the parents must control and change her. For such abusive parents, the elements of worthlessness, despair, rejection, and loss of positive relationships are more apparent.

MARITAL-PARENTING DYNAMICS

In many families where abuse occurs, there is also a high degree of marital conflict and general confusion in carrying out both marital and parental roles, probably a result of inadequately achieving Erikson's stage of identity. This force is an accumulation of the deficiencies and negative experiences in earlier stages of development, and the roots of dysfunction in both marital and parental relations are found within the other dynamics.

Within the marital roles, instability often results from the extreme dependency that both spouses feel for each other. Couples in abusive situations often convey an image of clinging desperately to each other to ward off external threats to their life-style. This is often a rationalization for the isolation that they maintain from the rest of their environment. In addition, this dependency and isolation often result in a relationship marked by roles which alternate between dominance and submissiveness.

In a number of cases, the abusive act is carried out by one spouse but takes place in the presence or invitation of the other spouse who plays a passive role. Because of the submissive spouse's own insecurities, fears of rejection, and loss of their only significant other, the spouse, he is unable to engage in firm limit setting. The abusive parents, whether actively or passively involved in the abusive act, are unable to move beyond their own needs and toward a realistic meeting of the needs of their child.

Although abusive parents have inadequate nurturing and negative life experiences, they have a tendency to marry into a situation similar to the one that they left, because this is an environment in which they are familiar. As a result, they often marry a spouse similar to their own parents. This reinforces their previous feelings about themselves, as well as the parenting skills learned from their own parents. Since abusive parents come from a negative environment, they are unable to achieve the stages of development necessary to be adequately functioning adults. They often live in an environment with another adult who has the same kind of characteristics. This union results in additional confusion in parental role identity.

Their basic sense of insecurity and their inability to move away from their own needs results in behavior that moves from overindulging either the spouse or the child, to angrily withdrawing from the relationship. In essence, there is often a complete inability to perceive one's self in the role of either positive spouse or of parent. There is rarely an opportunity for abusive parents to learn the giving role in a relationship, and the parents essentially receive rather than give nurturance.

SELF-CONCEPT

Abusive parents lack self-esteem which is reflected in their feelings of worthlessness and failure. Some abusive parents often behave on an impulsive by crisis basis, with little preplanning. This is often caused by a low frustration tolerance when dealing with environmental stresses. Others may react with overcontrol of themselves and others. This inability to express feelings in an appropriate way may result in outbursts of rage. On the other hand, there are instances where the parents reflect and assign responsibilities for life events to situations outside their control. In both situations, they feel helplessness in not being able to impact their environment and problem solving.

The acceptance of responsibility for one's own actions calls for maturity that stems from a mastery over Erikson's second stage, in which one develops a sense of autonomy. Abusive parents have often grown up in environments where there is little consistency or predictability. As children, they may cry often and sometimes their needs are met; other times they may be ignored; and other times they may be punished. Thus, they often have little ability to link cause and effect and to control themselves in a way that creates a sense of competency and order in their lives. Their negative self-concept and feelings of inadequacy further result in feelings of doubt and shame.

TRUST DYNAMICS

For many abusive parents, the world is an alien and inhospitable environment. This alienation is reflected not only in a general inability to engage in meaningful social relationships with other adults but is also reflected in the inability to engage meaningfully with their own children.

Abusive parents learn through prior inadequate socialization experiences that attachment relationships—even to their own parents—most often lead to rejection and disappointment. Thus, the abusive parents isolate themselves from others and fail to form supportive relationships which have the potential to provide positive input to them. Likewise, they feel the same mistrust toward their own child, as the establishment of close nurturing relationships with the child carries with it the risk of rejection and failure. As a result, the parents are unable to establish an appropriate attachment with their child. They are often unable to read the cues that their child's request or misbehavior provides. For example, if a child cries, the abusive parents often misread the cue and feel that the child does not like them and that they have failed as parents. The child will attempt to get his needs met in healthy ways; however, when nurturance is unavailable, he will withdraw or escalate his demands.

REFERENCES

1. Erikson, Eric H.: *Childhood and Society.* New York, W.W. Norton & Co., 1963.
2. Ibid., p. 247
3. Ibid., pp. 251-284
4. Ibid., p. 255
5. Ibid., p. 257
6. Ibid., pp. 258-260
7. Ibid., p. 260
8. Ibid., p. 261
9. Ibid., pp. 261-263
10. Steele, Brandt F., and Pollack, Carl B.: A psychiatric study of parents who abuse infants and small children. In Helfer, Ray E., and Kempe, C. Henry (Eds.): *The Battered Child.* Chicago, The University of Chicago Press, 1968, pp. 111-113.
11. Ibid., pp. 103-113

Chapter 3

THE INTERVENTION MODEL

FOR some time, researchers and clinicians have been attempting to make sense out of the concept of child abuse, its etiology, dynamics and therapy. Although much is known about abuse, there is little attempt to describe it within a theoretical framework.

Since Kempe's historical paper describing "The Battered Child Syndrome"[1] in 1962, there has been a plethora of research and program development geared to understanding child abuse, its consequences for the child and family, and the kinds of programs that would be helpful in combating the problem. Demographic variables have been investigated in the hope that certain characteristics of religion, income level, and age would be isolated to identify parents who abuse their children.[2] However, these variables have provided little information that would help to zero in on putting a stop to the problem.

The dynamics discussed in Chapter 2 point to the social aspects of the problem. Because role development is a significant variable and roles are learned, parenting behavior is viewed as being transmitted from generation to generation through the interaction of family members. It is fair to say, then, that the only way to control child abuse is through an intervention model that addresses these social characteristics. From this perspective the concept of socialization provides a basis for understanding, as well as for program development.

SOCIALIZATION

Brim suggests that socialization is the process through which persons acquire knowledge, skills, and attitudes that make them able members of society.[3] Knowledge, skills, and attitudes are the elements of roles, including parental roles, that are so important to everyday functioning and, consequently, societal functioning. Complete socialization enables persons to perform roles expected of them.

Socialization is a process, then, of social learning and occurs through interaction with others. Some people are more significant and, therefore, either more is learned from them, or what is learned from them is internalized more readily. In either case, there is some content transmitted to the learner.

A major component of socialization involves the learning of the role of the other. That is, in learning one's own role, one must also learn the complementary role in anticipating the other's response to one's own behavior. These complex interpersonal relationships are important in the development of self-concept, and parents are significant in this development.

An individual's socialization is also dependent upon the broader social and cultural context within which that person's interpersonal relationships occur. Factors such as poverty, employment opportunities, community support available to children and families, and national and community attitudes toward violence also impact on how individuals are socialized. For example, violence portrayed through the media, on television and in newspapers is a broad cultural phenomena deeply imbedded in American society, as is the parent's right to discipline their children. The limits of these two examples are not well defined and, therefore, excesses are a matter of subjective judgment.

Socialization into the parental role means, then, that the parental knowledge, skills, and attitudes toward self and others are learned throughout the child-rearing years. Attitudes are often the residue of a person's relationship with his own parents or significant others, as well as the impact of schools, television, and the type of community or neighborhood in which one was raised. What is being suggested here is that how a person parents is learned, and both appropriate and inappropriate parenting is transmitted and subsequently learned.

The following examples of complete and incomplete socialization may help to clarify what happens.

COMPLETE SOCIALIZATION. A young, mature, happily married couple decides to have children and plans for them. When they are born, the parents look on them and the events that surround their birth as very positive. In turn, they associate positive attributes of their children with themselves and their families. As the children grow, the parents anticipate their needs and capabilities, rewarding their achievements and surrounding them in an atmosphere of love and affection.

As the children grow and move further away from the family, they stand on their own. They are mature in their own right, having learned the tools for everyday living from their growing up or socialization. When the time comes, they seek out young individuals to date and perhaps eventually marry persons who grew up in a similar way, with similar maturity and security. The cycle repeats itself.

INCOMPLETE SOCIALIZATION. Two immature, self-centered young people marry and have children. Although initially the idea of having children is a happy thought, based in their desire for reciprocal love, ideas change as time passes and the negative cycle repeats itself. The children are born into an atmosphere of immaturity, unhappiness, and with many unmet needs. The children are not what the parents expected; in fact, they require care in response to their needs, instead of meeting the parents' needs. Each time the children want attention, the parents respond in a harsh, negative way.

As the children grow, it's not how well they are doing but why they could not do better. They are expected to care for themselves as well as to care for their parents. Their attributes are those of people not liked by mother or father, just as mother and father are not liked by their parents. The children may or may not be physically abused but they are ego abused, and, when the cycle repeats itself, they will look for spouses who are similar to themselves.

In summary, the socialization process not only provides the learning of knowledge and skills relative to parenting but also the attitudes about self and self relative to others. In the incomplete socialization process (that which takes place in abusive families), the end product is a child, and eventually an adult, who is immature, is unknowledgeable about appropriate methods for rearing children, is socially isolated from others, possesses a negative self-concept, lacks family solidarity, has unmet needs, and has many problems and an inability to problem solve.

THE RESOCIALIZATION MODEL

When incomplete socialization occurs resulting in the cycle of abuse, then the intervention model must take into consideration resocialization as a mechanism for breaking this cycle of abuse. The objective of intervention is to prepare the adult to be as mature as possible with the necessary knowledge, skills, and attitudes of parenting. It is a process of helping parents with a child abuse problem learn the parenting role. In resocializing, it is necessary to provide an atmosphere that can assist the individual with the resocialization process, which results in a mature role that did not exist in the beginning.

Resocialization can be conceptualized analytically to occur in three distinct stages of dependence, interdependence, and independence, or a developmental sequence of infancy through maturity. The model and objectives for each stage follows.

Dependence	Identity Crisis	Interdependence	Independence
Establish rapport	Question: "Who am I?"	Identify problems	Manage self
Begin to develop trust		Begin to problem solve	Interact with environment
Be a friend		Develop alternative patterns of behavior	Try new behaviors
Be a positive role model		Provide information	Reinforcement
Begin to provide information		Provide reinforcement for behavior	

Stage One: Dependence

The objective of stage one is to develop rapport with the parents. Since the parents lack a sense of trust and are suspicious of anyone they encounter, the helping person must move slowly and sincerely, such as friends deal with one another. The difference is that this relationship, for some time, is one-sided and takes tremendous energy on the part of the helper and continues to be one-sided until some rapport and trust is established. Then it is up to the helping person to make sure honesty, openness, and candor prevail. If the trust relationship is broken, it may never be reestablished.

When behavior is appropriate, the helping person reinforces the parent's behavior. At times, it is exceedingly difficult to find something positive to recognize, and it requires the helping person's talent and expertise to pick up on any opportunity that presents itself. In being a friend, the helping person is a positive role model. When behavior is negative, the helper is willing to point this out as well.

The consequence of stage one is the questioning on the part of the parents, Who am I? After all, no one was friends with the parents before, why now? The parents never trusted anyone before and no one ever cared. At this point, the parents want to revert back to the old ways, even though they have experienced the new. This ambivalence results in an identity crisis which is displayed as anxiety, frustration, hostility, confusion, and retreating to earlier behaviors. The function of the helping person is to continue exhibiting positive behaviors, reinforcing that the parents are worthwhile human beings. The parents move into stage two.

Stage Two: Interdependence

As soon as the parents start feeling positive about themselves and start developing a positive relationship with the helping person, they are ready to look at their problems. As they identify their problems, the helping person is able to help them sort through priorities and, when appropriate, suggest and discuss alternatives. Never, of course, should the helping person make decisions for the parents. This is the time when information is shared so the parents can replace old information with new and process it for its meaning. The key in stage two is for the helper to be available so that thoughts and actions that are appropriate can be positively reinforced.

During this stage, the helper assists the parents to meet basic needs by taking them to parenting classes or counseling. This also helps the parents interact with their larger society. This allows for the opportunity of positive interactions outside the home and problem solving in relation to making decisions about themselves. As the parents get more and more confident in their ability to manage, they need the helping person less and less, and the natural progression leads to stage three.

Stage Three: Independence

As the parents feel more confident in themselves and their surroundings, and as they realize they have some resources on which to rely, they are able to increasingly move outward and to attempt new ways of managing themselves and their environment. Consequently, the parents call upon the helping person less and need less and less reinforcement. One of the hazards in stage three is that the helping person may assess that the parents are able to manage on their own before they are ready. If support is withdrawn too soon, the parents will revert to dependency once again and it is more difficult to move them through the process. Often, just knowing someone cares is adequate support, with an occasional personal contact.

It would be helpful to be able to predict how long the process of resocialization takes, but we can only estimate. The length of time depends on the point at which the parents enter this relationship, their previous experiences with success and failure, and the intensity and commitment of the helping person. It may take one year or five. It is very difficult to predict.

However long it takes, it is important that the helping person understand the process and incorporate additional strategies into the therapeutic approach that will enhance the process. One strategy is to focus on the parents, not the child. Negative parenting behavior is the problem and the child is the recipient. If the helper focuses on the child, it may result in additional abuse to the child, since the parents may view the helper's attitude toward them as uncaring and negative.

The helper needs to be objective, understanding, and non-judgmental. The parents will know if the helping person has negative feelings about them. Teaching is more effective if it is by example rather than preaching. Information is shared in a comfortable, nonthreatening and nonjudgmental manner. Having parents demonstrate the new information and behaviors is an effective way to reinforce behaviors, as long as the response from the helper is objective and honest.

Another strategy that is important for the helper to understand reflects a principle of systems, of which the family can be considered. If one part of a system changes, it effects the rest of the system, since the system must adjust to the change. It is possible to change the entire dynamics by working with one person in the family. That does not mean that the helper never comes in contact with other family members. It does mean that if necessary the helper puts his energy into one relationship, not necessarily the perpetrator, and then interacts when possible with others.

Summary

Child abuse is conceptualized as a social problem that is transmitted from generation to generation through the learning of social roles. Parents tend to teach children to behave as they were taught. It is suggested that the way to stop the cycle of transmitting abuse is to teach abusers how to be productive parents and members of society. A resocialization model is suggested as that intervention program, which is the one adopted by SCAN. When combined with self-help groups, individual counseling and community support, the model is effective in its approach to treating the abusive family.

REFERENCES

1. Kempe, C. Henry et al., "The Battered Child Syndrome." *JAMA*, 191:17-24.
2. Gil, David G.: Incidence of child abuse and demographic characteristics of persons involved. In Helfer, Ray E., and Kempe, C. Henry (Eds.): *The Battered Child.* Chicago, The University of Chicago Press, 1968, pp.19-40.
3. Brim, Orville G.: Socialization through the life cycle. In Brim, Orville G., and Wheeler, Stanton: *Socialization after Childhood.* New York, John Wiley, 1966, p. 3.

Chapter 4

PUTTING THEORY INTO ACTION
The SCAN Treatment Modality

S CAN Volunteer Service, Inc. has developed a treatment modality which incorporates an overall framework suggesting that child abuse is best understood when viewed from a psychosocial and ecological model. This recognizes the psychological characteristics of parents, their prior life experiences, and their present living conditions and situational stresses.

The SCAN model primarily integrates three perspectives. The first is a holistic approach based on the premise that all individuals need acceptance and support as human beings. The second is an ego development approach, which suggests that because abusive parents did not receive appropriate emotional support during their childhood, they need to be taken back through the early developmental stages, such as those formulated by Erikson. These are stages in which individuals learn basic trust, how to achieve a sense of autonomy, and the fact that their behavior does impact their environment; a sense of initiative and the ability to problem solve; an ability to accomplish mastery over tasks undertaken; a sense of identity as an independent member of society; a sense of intimacy; and an ability to care for others. When individuals have not mastered the initial stages of human development satisfactorily, they have poor self-esteem, an inability to cope, and an incapacity to problem solve.

The third perspective is one of social control, or a behavioristic approach. This suggests that although individuals who abuse their children need empathy and support as they move through the intervention stages, they also need external control which states that child abuse is unacceptable. SCAN sets firm limits for parents. This limit setting helps parents develop alternate behaviors in interacting with their children and, consequently, they feel better about themselves.

The key elements of the treatment modality maintain that the principle focus of change is the parents feelings about themselves and the expectation that they can learn to control their behaviors, learn new behaviors, and stop abusing their children. The treatment provides opportunities to improve the parents' functioning and interaction as adults. The lay therapist takes the role of socializing agent, actively teaching, modeling, nurturing, sorting, limit setting, and problem solving, while she invites and waits for the participation of the parent. Within this process of treatment, the SCAN staff meets the parents at their level of need and provides support to them at their present developmental stage.

The lay therapist actively responds by acceptance of the parents. It is this process which leads to the establishment of trust. Although many treatment models require parents to begin problem solving immediately, it is the SCAN philosophy that the parents must first develop and establish attachment with the lay therapist. Thus, the lay therapist, through a one-to-one relationship invites the parents with a child abuse problem to develop trust, attachment, self-worth, confidence, and relationships with others outside the family. The task of the lay therapist is to develop a caring, noncritical, nonjudgmental relationship with the parents.

After the initial trust is developed, the lay therapist works with the parents in establishing some autonomy and ability to sort and problem solve. The parents look to the lay therapist as an effective role model who can teach parenting and problem-solving skills. During this whole process, the lay therapist provides reinforcement to the abusive parents that they cannot abuse their child and that such behavior is not to be tolerated. However, the lay therapist serves as a bail-out person and intervener to the parents to prevent abuse from occurring.

The SCAN treatment model for families involves a maturation process. This growth process may take several years. The SCAN volunteer lay therapist fosters a growth experience with the parents through their intervention. An extensive amount of time is spent each week in the home of their families.

The objectives that the model seeks to achieve with abusive families are: (1) intervention in the home as a bail-out person with the idea of ending parental isolation; (2) providing alternative child-rearing practices that replace the abusive behavior; (3) setting limits both for the parents and for the parents to set for the child; (4) modifying the parents' unrealistic expectations of the child's behavior; (5) changing the parents' self-image from negative to positive; (6) relieving home pressures which generally precipitate crisis; and (7) reparenting the parents.

When a child learns to swim, he usually makes a series of advancing steps gaining courage and enjoyment each time he gets nearer the water's edge. The families in the SCAN program do their own advancing toward water to find that the alternatives in parenting and living that they will learn can be safe and enjoyable for them. The lay therapist shows by modeling alternatives to the family that the world can be better. As children are encouraged to move closer to the goal of getting their feet wet, so are the parents supported and encouraged by the lay therapist. At first, families need constant reassurance from the lay therapist, and they will move and grow because they learn that the lay therapist is the teacher and the lifeguard.

Summary

This treatment model can be conceptualized as a three-stage process. The first stage is dependency, the second is interdependency, and the third is one of independence. In much the same way as we see healthy humans function after successful movement through developmental stages, this treatment model rests upon the premise that successful treatment must move in succession through the three stages. This treatment modality is based upon a way of looking at the parents' world and the developmental stages that exist.

CLARK CASE STUDY

Rachelle is a twenty-one-year-old woman, married with two young children, ages one and one-half and three. Recently, for a number of reasons, Rachelle and her husband, Robert, are experiencing severe stress. Rachelle was reported for abusing one of her children. Rachelle's story is typical of many parents.

Rachelle remembers her childhood as lonely with few friends. Although she lived with both of her parents, her father was a truck driver and was gone a great deal. Her mother spent the majority of her time with a younger brother who was continually sick. Rachelle married Robert at seventeen, who was just one year older, and they had two children within three years. Although Rachelle and Robert both say that they love their children a great deal, the children are often sick with ear infections, colds, and other ailments, and demand a great deal of attention. The family lives in a trailer in the country and has only one car. Robert, a laborer, works two jobs and is gone with the car the majority of the time. Thus, Rachelle is isolated at home, having only one close friend, a former high school classmate, who lives eight miles away.

Because of the numerous pressures, Rachelle and Robert have marital problems, which intensified when he lost one of his jobs. Although he is home more often, he feels stressed and is often short tempered. Rachelle states that he does not relate well to the children. During the time he is at home, he whips both children often with his belt for various reasons, none of which Rachelle thinks are deserving of such punishment.

After a fight with Robert, Rachelle screamed and hit her three-year-old when he spilled his soup. During the altercation, she pushed the child against the coffee table and he hit his head quite severely. He complained afterwards of being dizzy and began vomiting. Rachelle felt scared and took the child to the hospital.

Although this situation can happen anywhere in the country, fortunately, Rachelle lives in a community that has a unique child abuse intervention program. The hospital social worker immediately contacts SCAN Service, Inc.

The emergency room physician suspects that Rachelle and Robert Clark's son, Bob, is abused and he contacts the local SCAN office. Immediately, a SCAN staff evaluator goes to the hospital and meets with Rachelle and Robert Clark. Although

Mrs. Clark states that her husband has been beating the children with a belt, she claims that her son's head injury is an accident. However, she does admit that she is having problems with her marriage and her children. She is very receptive to receiving SCAN services, although she expresses fear and apprehension. The SCAN evaluator interviews both parents in a warm, accepting professional manner.

The next day the family is discussed in a community multidisciplinary team meeting. Those attending are: a SCAN staff member, physicians and nurses from the hospital, a psychologist, social service caseworker, a representative of a law enforcement agency, and a counselor from a child study center. It is recommended that the family be assigned to SCAN for services, a volunteer lay therapist be assigned to the family, and the family participate in Parents Anonymous. Part-time day care services are arranged for the children so that Mrs. Clark can have some time to meet her own needs. Later in treatment, the Clarks agree to participate in marriage counseling provided by the mental health agency.

While Bob is still in the hospital for further care and evaluation, the SCAN program staff identifies an appropriate volunteer.

Joan Thomas, a forty-three-year-old mother of four teenagers, and a former nurse, who has already successfully worked with a SCAN family is selected. The SCAN evaluator introduces Joan to the Clarks in a visit to their home. Although Joan provides the majority of services and support to the Clark family, many other individuals are involved in helping maintain and strengthen their family. Frequently, the SCAN supervisor meets with the Clarks at their home or in the office. She supervises Joan in case management at least twice weekly. She helps her realize the child abuse dynamics in the Clark family and she gives direction for Joan's interventions.

Since Joan first met the Clarks, she goes to their home every day and maintains telephone contact with Rachelle several times a day. This maximum amount of time is given due to the severity of the injury and the age of the injured child. Rachelle is somewhat apprehensive about establishing a relationship with a stranger. However, because of Joan's warmth, concern, and persistence, Rachelle begins to depend on her for assistance and support. Joan initially provides many concrete services. She takes Rachelle to visit Bob in the hospital and to observe a day care center. She helps Robert search for employment and she takes Robert and Rachelle to Parents Anonymous meetings. They spend many hours sorting and prioritizing the Clark's problems, feelings, and plans.

Joan also spends a great deal of time at the house with Rachelle. While she is there, Rachelle has the opportunity to observe Joan interacting with her children. They discuss her relationship with them, and Joan responds to many questions Rachelle has about child development and child rearing. Joan is asked to give Rachelle and Robert some concrete suggestions about some of the problems they are having with the children, for example, ways to deal with them at bedtime and mealtime.

After several months, when the Clarks develop a more trusting relationship with the lay therapist, and when they sort some of their problems, they agree to go to the mental health center for marriage counseling. They ask Joan to accompany them to the initial visit. They enjoy their session and join Joan for coffee afterwards. She learns that this is the first time they have been out together without the children in two years.

Joan arranges for the Clarks to receive food stamps. As time goes on, the Clarks do not seem to need as much of her time. However, about six months after SCAN started working with the family, Rachelle begins to feel very depressed and negative. She takes the children out of the day care center, is not home several times when Joan comes to the house, and hysterically calls one day saying that she has beaten her older child severely.

When Joan arrives at the home, she finds the child and Rachelle both very scared, but the child is unharmed. Joan provides intensive daily support for several weeks. She helps Rachelle sort through the issues which precipated the crisis.

Rachelle realizes that she has changed and she is liked and accepted by the SCAN staff, her Parents Anonymous friends, and is, in fact, a good wife and mother. She is able to work through her crisis. She then moves into a period of problem solving, and Joan helps her establish priorities and they begin to solve problems. She develops alternative methods of discipline, instead of feeling overwhelmed and abusing her child. As time goes on, Rachelle relies on Joan as a good friend whom she calls periodically, but she seems better able to cope with her stresses and her children.

During Joan's involvement with the Clarks, she goes to volunteer training programs every other week, when the volunteer cases are staffed, and she talks with other volunteers and staff about Rachelle. She receives ideas and hope as they discuss their families. A staff psychologist is available to the group for additional assistance, and Joan uses his ideas for guidance, particularly in approaching her suggestions to the Clarks that they need further counseling. The Clarks are also staffed by the multi-disciplinary team so that all of the community services can be coordinated.

When Rachelle's son tells her how much he likes her because she does not hit or hurt him anymore, Rachelle calls Joan to share this with her and Joan brings her a flower so that they can share Rachelle's excitement and pleasure. As Rachelle summarizes it at a SCAN training session, I feel good about where I am and who I am. The kids and everyone else used to control my life, but now I know that if I feel rage and want to hurt Bob, I can call SCAN and Joan before I do something that I will regret.

Chapter 5

IMPLEMENTING THE RESOCIALIZATION
APPROACH WITH ABUSIVE PARENTS
Dependent Stage

My mother never held me, I don't
know how to hold Helen.
I put him in his room for six hours and
he pitched a fit, why is he so bad?
She looked at me funny ever since she was born.
I know she is only two, but she stole my money.
I thought that feeling guilty was what all
parents felt.
It cries to get even with me.
I'm such a bad mother.
She rocks too loud. I am afraid
I am going to hurt her.

THESE are statements made by parents who were in treatment
at SCAN. Their pain and confusion are obvious. They bene-
fited from treatment and became safe with their children. However,
these parents were allowed ample time to progress through the dependency stage.

The dependency stage of treatment is the initial stage that immediately follows the abusive act. For individuals such as Rachelle
Clark, it is the period of highest depression and greatest emotional
suffering. First, childhood, and now parenthood, is filled with

unhappy experiences. The act of the abuse and treatment with social agencies are further indications to the parents that they are a total failure. The lay therapist thus begins involvement with parents at a time when invariably strong emotions are present. Parents may express hostility, fear or passivity. All of the conflicting, ambivalent feelings the parents have about themselves, about their own parents, about their success or failure as parents and as people are exhibited. The parents feel confused, afraid, ashamed, alarmed, and in the midst of strangers who have the power to take their children from them.

The goal of treatment in the dependency stage is to start reparenting the parents. This stage allows for growth as opposed to pathological dependency. The parents begin learning new behaviors and new coping skills. This part of treatment is very time consuming and emotionally draining for the lay therapist and the SCAN staff. There is not a predetermined amount of time that parents take to move through this stage. Some parents may experience more nurturing in their lives and be able to be interdependent sooner, while others need to be allowed to be dependent for many months.

In this stage and in all stages of treatment, the dynamics of abuse and the characteristics of the parents that lead to abuse must be dealt with by the parents and program staff. It is important for the program staff to choose the appropriate lay therapist for the family. For example, some lay therapists understand the dynamics of the battered child syndrome, while others are more effective with parents who refer themselves for services. The task of the lay therapist is to help the parents establish a positive, trusting relationship. The lay therapist and staff's attitude toward the parents must be caring, nonjudgmental and noncritical. The message given to the parents over and over is that the lay therapist cares about them, that they are worthwhile, that they have done good parenting, and that the lay therapist and parents can think together about how to solve their problems.

The lay therapist accepts the parents warmly and empathetically, yet openly and honestly. She accepts the parents as people, however, she does not condone negative or abusive behavior. The lay therapist is saying by her consistent visits to the home that she wants to spend time with the parents. This stage requires much nurturing energy that is free of rivalry and seduction.

In the first weeks of visiting, the lay therapist spends many hours listening to the parents, as most abusive parents seem to need to reiterate their life story. Other parents who are more passive and who resist communication are more difficult to work with initially. The lay therapist reminds the parents that she and the staff are on call to the parents twenty-four hours a day, seven days a week, in case of an emergency. She encourages the parents to call if they feel abusive toward their child. She emphasizes how important it is to call before abusing their child, since abusive parents have a tendency to wait until after the act of violence to reach out for help. The lay therapist leaves her phone number on each visit, and she encourages the parents to locate a nearby telephone that they can use if they do not have one.

> Donna called the SCAN office saying that she felt extremely angry and that she was going to hurt her four-year-old son. A lay therapist went immediately to her home and brought Donna to the office. The staff told her that they would take care of her son, Billy. They encouraged her to go do something good for herself. Late in the afternoon Donna came back to the office expressing excitement. She related that she spent all day alone at the zoo. She explained that this was her first day of having fun in years. Billy was safe to go home.

In this stage, the work is intensely parent oriented. By focusing on the parents, the lay therapist does not invite feelings of jealousy or anger from the parents to the child. For example, a day care staff member directed an abusive parent to keep her child cleaner. The mother politely agreed. She hysterically called SCAN hours later after trying to drown her child. She finally explained that the child had made her look like a bad parent.

The lay therapist does examine the children during each visit and she observes to make sure the children's needs are being met. She may hold the child, yet she still concentrates on the parent. She observes interactions of the parents and children and carries out recommendations of the professional staff regarding any community resources that the children might need, such as medical evaluation, psychological evaluation, and day care.

Sometimes in the early stages of treatment, protecting a child's life and safety is the immediate concern. A petition for temporary custody of the child or children is made to the juvenile or family court. This decision is based upon the age of the child, the severity of the injuries, and the cooperation, or lack of cooperation, of the parents. Court action is therapeutic for some parents who need strong limits. It is important for these parents to realize that society, represented by the court, will not tolerate their behavior and that violence is unacceptable.

Parental hostility and denial of responsibility are difficult to penetrate because of the parents' overwhelming fear of prosecution and/or loss of the child permanently. Many parents do not understand the meaning of temporary foster care and do not believe that the court or agency is there to help them.

The court hearing is usually the most frightening time for the parents and they often do not hear all that is said. The lay therapist can be an invaluable support emotionally, someone safe to whom the parents can express anger, and someone to replay what the judge and the witnesses said when the parents are more willing to hear. Since the staff and professionals are the persons providing the testimony, the lay therapist has the opportunity to support the parents and express the idea that now is the time to get on with changes in their lives.

The lay therapist concentrates on helping the parents meet concrete needs. She encourages the parents to ask for ideas and assistance in the management of home and children. She praises small successes of parents and watches for any change in behavior to praise. She helps parents who are experiencing financial problems, obtain food stamps, arrange for public assistance, locate day care centers and babysitting services, and obtain legal services if needed. She may assist in locating housing, job training, and transportation. Many parents have neglected these tasks before, because of disorganized living standards or because of fear they associate with seeking help from outside agencies.

The continued presence of the lay therapist, the accomplishment of completing some of the concrete tasks, and the solving of some of the initial problems begin to effect the parents' self-concept. Some parents show a change in their self-concept by changing their appearance, such as Trudy. Trudy's lay therapist concentrated most of her time on Trudy's relationship with her child. Trudy's change was obvious when she and her son openly showed affection toward one another. She had her hair cut and styled, lost ninety pounds, and even went to a make-up consultant. She found ways for the family to have transportation and new activities. When she spoke on a Parents Anonymous panel, she reviewed her life story and read a poem for her lay therapist which described where her anger could have lead her if she had not been reported for child abuse.

The parents see an individual who shows them that they are liked, that being with them is enjoyable and that small successes are not beyond their reach. The parents' sense of isolation will start to diminish. They may thoroughly enjoy the regular telephone conversations and visits with the lay therapist, relishing in the attention. Parents report that in many instances their lay therapist and professional staff have brought them their first flowers, made their first birthday cake, brought them their first gift, and provided other aspects of attention that many normally functioning individuals take for granted or see to be insignificant.

Although the lay therapist provides the primary services in the home, the parents are encouraged to drop into the SCAN office whenever possible. The SCAN office conveys a family atmosphere of informality and friendliness. Gifts that parents bring to staff are displayed on walls and shelves. Some parents bring their child with a blanket and toy and stay in the office for hours. They seem to feel safe and enjoy the warmth.

In addition, parents may be involved in attending weekly meetings of Parents Anonymous, a parent self-help group consisting of other abusive parents, who share similar life experiences and needs. The lay therapist assists in Parents Anonymous often by encouraging the parents to attend, arranging for child care, or transporting the parents to the meetings with a special stop for coffee or relaxation prior to or after the meeting.

The lay therapist often encourages the parents to reach out to other community resources which parents previously felt too insecure to accept. As they begin to learn that treatment program staff and the lay therapist are trustworthy, parents begin to trust back and start meeting their own needs. This helps to establish and reinforce the strength and quality of the relationship.

During the dependency stage, the lay therapist must establish limits for the parents, saying that they cannot continue to abuse their child; it is alright to feel angry, but they cannot hurt another person. She encourages the parents to express anger in a different manner by yelling at a tree, slugging away at a pillow, running round the house, or jumping up and down. The parents are directed to call the lay therapist before abusing their child. The lay therapist states that the parents may not abuse their child and that she is willing to work with them and to help them think of other ways to deal with their child.

Also, it is important for the lay therapist to set limits regarding her time. When the parents call the lay therapist at an inconvenient time, she states that she cannot talk but that she is willing to call back at a designated time. It is good modeling for the parents to experience the lay therapist keeping her word by calling back at the agreed upon time. The lay therapist responds immediately if the parent has a legitimate emergency.

The lay therapist and treatment program staff also become models and teachers of good parenting. The lay therapist starts teaching the parents good child management and appropriate means of discipline. Abusive parents need many alternatives to abuse. The lay therapist spends much of the time discussing with the parents the capabilities of the children based on their age and developmental stage. They discuss ways of communicating verbally, instead of physically. At this point, the lay therapist can do a great deal of modeling with the children to help the parents understand positive parenting practices.

Abusive parents have a lot of misinformation about children, so information giving is critical. Some questions asked by parents may be:

- What can a three-year-old do for himself?
- How can I potty train my kid?
- What do I do when he won't eat?

The lay therapist may point out where the parents' expectations are unrealistic for the child. She may give information or examples to the parents such as:

- Children respond to praise.
- One option is to send Bob to his room for five minutes. You can set your timer and he will hear it go off. Will you do that the next time he misbehaves?
- Babies give us cues when they cry, since they may be wet, hungry, or just lonesome.
- When you hold Mike, he will enjoy your looking into his eyes.
- Babies like to be held and cuddled when they nurse. Propping the bottle is dangerous.

As staff and lay therapist praise the parents and point out tasks completed and behavior changes made, the parents begin to see themselves as unique. Also, the lay therapist praises the child to the parents and extensively points out the child's abilities and personality traits. This helps the parents start seeing themselves and their child as separate human beings. Many times when the child is literally separate from the parents, by being in day care, the parents are more willing to establish separateness. A well-trained day care director or counselor can describe a child's needs and capabilities to the parents. They can explain what kind of activities the child is benefiting from in the class and to what type of positive attention he responds. The parents start understanding that their child is not the person to meet their needs.

The lay therapist and treatment staff also encourage abusive parents to relax and enjoy some recreation. Many abusive parents have little fun in their lives because they think they are either inadequate or undeserving. Since they were abused as children, many parents never observed any family member having fun. Parents report that the first time they ever have any kind of social activity is through the treatment program. The lay therapist and treatment staff learn what the parents consider to be relaxing recreation and assist the parents in arranging for it. Simple games such as playing a game of ball with the entire family is good modeling. Picnics are enjoyed by staff, lay therapists and families.

The staff also assists the parents in developing reliable bail-out systems, first through the lay therapist and later through other community resources. Healthy coping adults rely on numerous people when they are under stress, when their paycheck is late, when their baby gets sick, or when the car breaks down. The lay therapist assists the parents in learning appropriate ways to cope successfully with stressful situations. She explains that other people can help and, most importantly, that other people do care and want to provide assistance.

During the dependency stage of treatment, contact with the parents is as frequent as possible — at least several times a week. The dependency process means caring for the family members, setting limits, assisting with concrete tasks, teaching child management and parenting skills, providing information, and being an available friend. The SCAN view of treatment is that reparenting must start at the onset of treatment and that the parents must meet their nurturing, dependency needs. Physical and emotional support are critical in helping the parent accomplish this growth. Parents must have a realistic understanding of their children's capabilities, and the program staff must have realistic expectations of the families with whom they are working.

Chapter 6

IMPLEMENTING THE RESOCIALIZATION
APPROACH WITH ABUSIVE PARENTS
The Identity Crisis

I do not know who I am anymore.
I know I was a bitch all my life.
My mother told me so.
I do not know who I am anymore.
That SCAN person thinks I am okay.
Hell, I don't know.
I failed my job on purpose.
I feel bad again like I used to.
I have always been a failure.

THESE are quotes from abusive parents who are experiencing the identity crisis. At some point before moving into the interdependent stage, most abusive parents go through an identity crisis. This identity crisis occurs because the parents do not recognize themselves in relation to their newly emerging behaviors. While in the past they saw themselves negatively, the abusive parents are now developing relationships and are beginning to be seen positively by others and by themselves. This shift from a negative to a more positive image leads to an agonizing questioning about their identities.

The parents state concerns that they may slip back to old behaviors and sometimes want to repeat negative behaviors. This regression gives the answer to, "Who am I?" Although the new behavior is positive, the thought of being able to maintain it and accept unknown consequences is frightening. The old, familiar behavior is not as threatening. The parents attempt to establish their original position of being a failure. They remember how much more comfortable they felt being rejected. Many parents once had unloving, uncaring, unsupportive, and even abusive parents themselves. When they turned to their mothers and fathers for love, they were rejected or abused. Their need for nurturing was unsatisfied and met with neglect or violence. They grew up knowing that the people they wanted to love were destructive.

The lay therapist demonstrates her understanding and concern for the parents over and over again. If the parents start to feel close to the lay therapist and reveal their need for love, friendship, and attention, there is a natural recall to the past. The parents begin to think that the lay therapist will leave them and so they begin to throw little boomerangs into the relationship or behave in such a way as to encourage the lay therapist not to like them. During this stage the parents, not unlike a rebellious adolescent, may break an appointment, quit a job, remove children from day care, and express continual dissatisfaction with the lay therapist.

An articulate parent made significant progress through the dependency stage. She was very verbal with members of Parents Anonymous and SCAN staff. However, one day she came to the SCAN office looking depressed and unkept. She lost her job because she refused to be at work on time and as a result she had to move to a cheaper apartment. The day care center reported that the children were coming to school tired, unfed, and possibly abused.

The treatment staff expressed their concern to Sandy and even gave her the option of placing her children in foster care. She was very critical of any suggestions and resisted the lay therapist's caring. She remained depressed for weeks, until one day she appeared in the SCAN office. She related how frightened she felt with her newfound successes, how she never had her life in order, and how she wanted to make her supporters leave her alone. She felt frightened because she did not think she could maintain her new image. She explained how she set up each one of her recent failures. She then stated that she had made a decision not to be a victim but to take charge of her life.

It is not unusual during this stage of treatment for the parents to confess to incidences of reabuse. Treatment program staff report that there is a significant change in the severity of the abuse when it does occur. For example, the parents may confess to whipping the child severely, when, upon investigation, the child has a hand spanking on the buttocks. At this point, the lay therapist and other staff help the parents see that their change is still positive and that progress is being made. This incidence is part of the testing period. The lay therapist's role is to reaffirm their acceptance of the parents, while not condoning the abusive behavior.

It is valuable to realize that the growth in the parents' trusting capacity and the strides made in coping and in accepting appropriate help will be assimilated at some point, but that the assimilation process takes time. Like the adolescent, the parents need to test their boundaries, but they need help in drawing the boundaries. For example, a parent was told to discipline her child by putting him in his room. At the next meeting the parent related how she put the child in his room for six hours and that the staff was wrong in their ideas. From this test the staff learned to suggest very specific alternatives to the parents and to ask the parents what their understanding is of the alternatives.

This stage is particularly difficult for treatment programs and at this time protective service staff might drop families from their caseload. With this they reinforce the stereotype belief that parents are not able to change. When this stage is not understood, they may recommend severing parental rights needlessly. It is important for the supervisory staff to be involved in providing additional supportive services to the parents. The lay therapist may interpret the identity crisis as her own failure. Thus, the lay therapist benefits from a great deal of supervision from the professional staff and support from other lay therapists. The lay therapist is encouraged to continue providing intensive supportive services as she did during the dependency stage.

During the identity crisis, staff and the lay therapist must help the parents to see that there has been change, that progress is being made, and that the trusting relationships already established will be maintained. When the lay therapist continues to go to the home of the parents, in spite of the parents' expression of hostility and rejection toward them, the parents realize that they are still worthwhile and important. The lay therapist can review the actual client record with the parents to point out how much progress the family has made.

The parents must have continual reassurance that they have not slipped back into their old patterns but are still in a growth process. They need help in sorting their feelings of confusion. The lay therapist continues to set limits, reaffirm the parents' self-worth, invite goal setting, and continues to care. This stage of intervention is critical. If the parents' regression is reinforced by the lay therapist's withdrawal, the parents will then have proven their original belief: that they are no good and that people do not care.

Chapter 7

IMPLEMENTING THE RESOCIALIZATION APPROACH WITH ABUSIVE PARENTS
Interdependent and Independent Stages

THE INTERDEPENDENT STAGE

PARENTS with a child abuse problem give clues to the staff that they are entering the interdependent stage. The parents might say:

. I feel good about myself.

I decided to get a job at the construction company.

I talked to my Parents Anonymous friend and she helped me decide to go to beauty school.

We are going out tonight with our family.

These statements tell us that the parents are reaching out to others to break their isolation. They are indicating that they are ready to start solving their own problems. Previously, the lay therapist has been the parents' bail-out person; now, the community will be the parents' bail-out system.

This interdependent stage of treatment reflects a movement of the intervention from a less affective nurturing level to a more cognitive level. It is during this stage that the parents begin progress from being influenced by external controls to developing internal controls. Thus, the parents are now more independent in developing appropriate coping behaviors. Behavior of the parents is marked by less impulsivity and more appropriate control. Parents begin to take a more thoughtful and planned approach to deal with life situations. For example, a parent relates how he decided to go for a walk instead of striking his child.

During this stage, the parents define most of their own problems. The lay therapist encourages the parents to verbalize possible solutions to problems and then waits for them to choose an appropriate answer. It is important to point out to the parents the consequences of some of their options. This direction assists the parents in understanding cause and effect, which is critical for their effective problem solving in future relationships. For example, one parent stated that he planned to buy a new car and move to a nicer house. The staff member asked him how much money he was making monthly. From the discussion, he decided he did not have enough money for both and decided on the house.

The parents gradually use the lay therapist less to provide answers and more as a sounding board. This process is reflective of Erikson's stage of development focusing on autonomy. From this sense of autonomy will come positive feelings within the parents of being able to master problems. A particular focus during this stage is the development of more advanced child management skills.

The interdependent stage is a satisfying one for both parents and lay therapist. Information giving is particularly important and effective. The relationship between parents and lay therapist is more comfortable and relaxed, and contact with the parents is somewhat decreased. In this stage, the parents nurture their child and see their child as separate from themselves. The big step that one parent reports is when she saw her child as a person with feelings, too. The lay therapist provides a great deal of positive reinforcement to the parents when new, more appropriate behaviors are employed.

Much of SCAN's efforts during this stage are to assist the parents to move toward other individuals and resources. Parents are encouraged to seek out and to use community services that they need and to begin to expand their support systems, so that in future crisis they will be able to reach out to an enlarged bail-out system.

The parents use their relationship with the lay therapist to help build relationships with other people. The lay therapist encourages the parents to become involved in groups and to make contact with other helpers and support systems. Many parents come to the

SCAN office and request information about where they can go for marriage counseling or where schooling is available. In addition, they ask how to get an appointment, how long they have to wait, what they can expect, and ask for approval of their decision.

This is the time to emphasize parenting classes, Parents Anonymous, and psychological counseling. The parents will now derive the most benefit from these services. Parents who have chosen psychological counseling have shown us that therapy related to changing pathological behavior is complementary to the SCAN program when the parent is in the interdependent stage.

In many instances, parents begin to use their skills and experiences with the treatment program to establish relationships and assist new parents coming into the treatment program and Parents Anonymous. Parents at this time begin to move toward community support systems such as church groups, newly befriended neighbors, and friends of their children. For example, when the Murphy family came to Parents Anonymous the first night, they were so hostile that staff members felt frightened and asked one of the parents to talk with the Murphys. One parent willingly explained SCAN and Parents Anonymous and pointed out to Mr. Murphy the benefits of the program.

Many times parents with a child abuse problem believe that no one else in the world abuses their children. When the parents are able to express their feelings in group meetings with other abusive parents, they show great relief that someone else has had some of the same feelings and experiences. Parents benefit from permission given by other parents, such as it is alright to put your child in day care, it is alright to get angry at your husband, and it is alright for you not to have another baby. Additional benefits come from sharing helpful hints on child-rearing practices.

The building of relationships beyond SCAN services expands the basic sense of trust that the parents are developing toward their environment. In addition to being willing to take greater responsibility for their actions, parents become better able to engage in giving relationships. The parents during the latter part of this stage begin to show a more appropriate balance of their behavior and are able to engage in giving as well as receiving. They take on more appropriate adult roles and behaviors.

Judy was reported to SCAN for abusing one of her six children. She had been abandoned by her mother as an infant and was moved from family member to family member. When her mother visited Judy she always called her an old hag. SCAN had worked with Judy for an extended period of time when her neighbor was reported for neglect to another protective service agency. The helping agency had threatened to remove the neighbor's children. Judy called her SCAN lay therapist and pleaded with her to come and show her friend what to do with her children. Judy stated that she would help her friend to take care of the children.

THE INDEPENDENT STAGE

The independent stage is considered the stage of stabilization in the treatment process. At this point, the parents have a greater sense of self-esteem and establish reasonable limits on behavior both for themselves and their child. Their functioning is more stable and more enjoyable, and their perception of the world is more positive and safe for them. Mistakes are usually aborted, but if they are made, they do not have the damaging impact that they had previously. They are able to stand criticism better and act upon it. Instead of criticism being seen as devastatingly threatening, it is viewed as input for consideration for possible growth.

During this stage, the parents recognize their own emotional needs and find resources to fulfill these needs. Inner family relationships are strengthened. The parents are willing to look at their own parents with closure on the past associated guilt or hatred. Within this stage, the parents begin to develop a basic sense of intimacy, finalizing the successful movement from the childhood stages of development to those stages associated with adulthood. For example, Marilyn was a very angry parent who talked incessantly. She spent hours in bed ignoring her children's behavior. Periodically, she struck her young daughter out of rage. After months of treatment, she decided she needed to resolve her resentment toward her mother. She left the state to visit her mother and attempted to reconcile their relationship. When she returned, she stated that she realized she would never get the nurturing that she longed for from her mother. She began to reach out and ask for acceptance from other parents and her lay therapist.

As the parents move through the independent stage, they need less intervention. The staff sees the parents once a week, then twice a month, and then once a month. They are reassured many times by the treatment staff that they can return to their lay therapist and to SCAN at any time. Treatment program staff report numerous instances where parents have not been seen for several years and then they will call during a crisis and need some additional support. Often, this support is just a phone call during one emotionally down evening.

> Mary called a staff member and related that she was responding to stress as she had done in the past. She verbalized that even though she was working, she was in an unhealthy situation. She resigned her position and found a new place of employment. She stated she had lived in chaos before but that she did not have to do so again.

> Susie related a similar story, saying that she needed assistance in finding a physician to regulate her medication. In the past she had experienced extreme emotional dysfunctioning, but she had come to the place of recognizing when she was in trouble.

> Another exciting phone call happened when a teenager helped his mother make a long distance call to ask a staff member for ideas. The parent was experiencing a lot of stress, and the teenager remembered SCAN from when his parents were clients when he was five years old.

Treatment program staff do not ever sever the relationship per se but are always available if the parents wish to reestablish services. In many instances, the parents remain in contact and they often drop in or call to share new and exciting experiences in their lives. Friendships do not need to be terminated. The amount of contact between friends can change, as well as the intensity of the relationship.

Chapter 8

SCAN VOLUNTEER SERVICE, INC.

S CAN Volunteer Service, Inc. is a private non-profit agency contracted through Arkansas Social Services on 55 percent Title XX monies, 25 percent state appropriation, and 20 percent community donor money. SCAN is a comprehensive community-based program that provides supportive services to families who abuse their children. In 1984, this program is in operation in fifteen Arkansas counties. The program serves approximately 4,400 clients a year.

SCAN receives reports of suspected child abuse and neglect occuring within fifteen SCAN counties, investigates reports of abuse and severe neglect, and provides intensive services to children under twelve and their families in cases where reports of abuse are substantiated. Families where the abuse occurs to children over twelve, or where neglect is substantiated are referred to the local office of the state social service agency.

SCAN provides services to families through four components: professional staff, trained lay therapists, parenting education, and Parents Anonymous. SCAN works in close coordination with Arkansas Social Services, the courts and other community agencies. Hospital multi-disciplinary teams help to ensure their coordination.

HISTORY

The SCAN program began in 1972 when its founder and executive director befriended a young woman and her child in a drugstore in Little Rock. Ms. Pallone recognized that the woman was having a number of problems. She later learned that the parent was fleeing from another state on a child abuse charge. Ms. Pallone spent a number of months working with the woman on a volunteer basis providing assistance, including support, nurturing and guidance, direction, transportation, seeking housing and employment, and advocating for her needs.

As a result of this single situation, a local psychiatrist suggested that Ms. Pallone locate other volunteers who could provide similar services to abusive parents. SCAN Volunteer Service, Inc. was begun with its files housed in the trunk of Ms. Pallone's car. From that initial effort, SCAN has grown yearly.

Six volunteers were recruited and trained and became the nucleus of SCAN, which was incorporated a few months later in order to negotiate a contract with Arkansas Social Services. The contract provided $40,000 funding to pay the salaries of the director and secretary, office expenses, and a $50 monthly reimbursement for the initial 25 lay therapists.

As SCAN staff and volunteers worked with abusive parents, the staff of the local medical center, the hospitals and other community resources began to make additional referrals to SCAN and became advocates for the program. In 1973, the SCAN contract was expanded to provide services in three additional counties. Also, in 1973, SCAN and Arkansas Social Services were awarded a three-year demonstration grant from the Office of Child Development, Health, Education and Welfare, which allowed for additional program expansion within those three counties.

ORGANIZATION

Although SCAN initially was founded by one individual, it became a rapidly expanding agency, both geographically and in comprehensiveness of service. Thus, from necessity, SCAN evolved into an organizational structure which allows for flexibility in accomplishing both administrative and service delivery tasks.

Board of Directors

SCAN is governed by a board of directors which develops broad goals and establishes general agency policy. The board also plays a strong leadership role in fund raising, relating to the state legislature, and developing and strengthening relationships with other agencies. The board includes eighteen community representatives, including one lay therapist, and one staff member, with the executive director as the ex officio member. Professions represented are: attorneys, accountants, social workers, physicians, nurses, ministers, school administrators, and social service representatives.

State Office Administration Staff

The executive director is responsible for implementing the directions and policies established by the board; providing the overall day-to-day administration and operation of the agency; negotiating funding contracts and interagency agreements; and overseeing case management, training, and case decisions by the agency. She also serves as the primary spokesperson for SCAN, interacting with the state legislature and maintaining positive public relations. The executive director directly supervises the three state program directors, who meet weekly to ensure coordination, joint planning, and decision making. The executive director is also the executive director of SCAN America, Inc.

The state director oversees SCAN services to clients. This includes management of SCAN cases, including final decisions regarding foster care placement and court action. She supervises four state coordinators who provide the linkage between the central office and the fifteen individual SCAN counties.

The state director of program operations administers day-to-day personnel and fiscal policies on a statewide level, supervises state clerical staff, and is responsible for developing and implementing program evaluations to ensure compliance of program standards. The state director of training and education is responsible for developing and implementing community awareness efforts, educational programs for professionals, and all staff training activities. This includes the initial training for lay therapists, in-service training for both lay therapists and staff, and advanced training for staff.

The state coordinators are responsible for supervising one to three county directors, depending on the population of the counties and the size of the caseload in each county. The state coordinators meet as a group weekly with state office administrative staff and are responsible for implementing policy and program decisions within each county to ensure program continuity. State coordinators provide a primary role in coordinating with local community agencies, particularly district offices of social services, the court, and local law enforcement officials.

SCAN Community Offices

Each SCAN office has a director, an assistant director, and one or more evaluators. In counties with smaller caseloads, the role of the evaluator is often filled by the assistant county director. SCAN program staff at the state and county levels have experiences from community agencies and many have master's degrees in social work and former experience in child protective services. Each county also includes at least one clerical position.

The SCAN county director supervises all county level staff and is responsible for overseeing the implementation of:

(1) an appropriate investigation of reports of child abuse and neglect within the county and appropriate decisions regarding cases;

(2) the recruitment, screening, training, and case assignment of lay therapists;

(3) appropriate management of all cases, including the supervision of lay therapists and the coordination of services required by clients;

(4) ensuring that SCAN program components operate in the county with maximum effectiveness and follow the overall SCAN policies, procedures, and the treatment approach.

The SCAN county assistant director or evaluator is responsible for investigating abuse and neglect cases when a referral is received from any resource.

Lay Therapists

A significant component of the SCAN program is the services to families provided by the lay therapists. These are trained volunteers who provide one-to-one supportive in-home services to families in the SCAN program. The SCAN program staff carefully supervises the lay therapists, who carry from one to five cases, with an average of three. It is the lay therapist's responsibility to establish a trust relationship with the family; to assist the family in obtaining resources; to help the family meet concrete needs; and to provide extensive interventions based on the treatment model.

Other Staff and Consultants

When funding permits, a clinical psychologist is on the SCAN staff and provides individual and group counseling, as well as case consultation. An attorney is retained and represents SCAN in legal actions.

Psychological, legal, and other services are also available at the county level to local SCAN staff as needed. A number of consultants participate in the SCAN system; these include physicians, psychiatrists, registered nurses, psychologists, financial and management consultants, child development specialists, and educational specialists.

The organizational structure continually emphasizes that the primary focus of the SCAN program is on the family with a child abuse problem, and on the lay therapist. Both receive a great deal of support from the SCAN staff.

Formal communication is facilitated by frequent staff meetings, training sessions, and case staffings. Unique aspects of the agency are its informal communication system and its warm, supportive, and totally client-oriented atmosphere. SCAN offices maintain a family centered environment where parents, their children, and lay therapist can visit and receive a friendly reception and encouragement.

SERVICES

The SCAN program proposes four major components. First, the lay therapist provides the majority of supportive services to parents in the home, with close supervision by SCAN staff. They provide a one-to-one supportive relationship to individual families, being available twenty-four hours a day, seven days a week.

The second component, Parents Anonymous, is a parent self-help group organized nationally with local chapters throughout the country. Most local SCAN offices have an active Parents Anonymous chapter. The chapter meets weekly and is coordinated by a Parents Anonymous sponsor, who is a SCAN staff member or may be a person from another community agency. The sponsor sees that arrangements are made for meetings, that membership is consistent by providing support to members, and by serving as a facilitator during chapter meetings. Babysitting and transportation are provided by SCAN for Parents Anonymous meetings.

The lay therapist also plays a major role in aiding parents in joining Parents Anonymous, as they are often apprehensive about joining the group. As parents move into the interdependent stage of the treatment process, they often develop supportive relationships with others that they meet in Parents Anonymous and form their own mutual helping network.

The third component, parent education, provides parenting education groups for parents who abuse their children. Groups are led by SCAN staff, as well as consultants from the community. Child development and child-rearing attitudes and practices are included in these group sessions, as well as sharing with other parents. This often provides parents with a more realistic understanding of their own children. The lay therapist assists the parent by encouraging attendance, providing transportation, and arranging child care if needed.

The fourth component, the multi-disciplinary team, is usually a hospital-based team which is designed to review families whose child has been admitted to a hospital as a result of an inflicted injury. SCAN recommends the following as team members: physicians, nurses, psychologists, law enforcement representatives, attorneys, social service representatives, SCAN representatives, and any other interested professionals.

PROGRAM PROCESS

When a report of child abuse is received at a local SCAN office, it is referred to a staff member performing intake duties. The staff member completes an intake form with information about the family, and supervisory staff decide whether SCAN should conduct an investigation. This decision is based upon written guidelines developed jointly by SCAN and social services. If the case is not appropriate for SCAN, the family is referred to an appropriate agency. All reports received by SCAN are discussed in staff meetings held daily. All reports are sent to Arkansas Social Service district offices and to the State Central Child Abuse and Neglect Registry.

If the report is appropriate for SCAN, a SCAN evaluator investigates. The SCAN investigation includes an interview with the referral source; a home visit to evaluate the family; a complete medical examination of the children; and interviews with other individuals who may have knowledge about possible abuse or neglect within the family. Written reports of all investigations are sent to the district social service offices, to the State Central Registry, and to the local law enforcement agency.

Once an investigation is completed, the case is presented at one of the daily staff meetings, and a case decision is made by the professional staff. The staff may decide upon a number of alternatives:

(1) if the abuse report is unconfirmed, SCAN may take no further action;

(2) the case is referred to the state agency if it is inappropriate for SCAN services — for example, if it is an abuse case of a child over twelve or a non-life-endangering neglect situation;

(3) the case may be opened by SCAN without legal action;

(4) SCAN may work with social services in petitioning the court for a hearing or for emergency removal of a child if the child is in a life-threatening situation. Placement of the child in a foster home is accomplished by social services. SCAN works with the family to reunite the family as quickly as possible.

(5) SCAN may work with the state agency in petitioning the court for a supervisory order for social services to obtain legal supervision of the child or to require specific actions by the family while the child remains in the home; or

(6) SCAN may deliver crisis services and refer the case to a more appropriate agency when the crisis subsides. These crisis services are usually provided by SCAN staff rather than a lay therapist.

If a case is accepted by SCAN, a written plan is developed by the staffing team for review with the family. The case is assigned to a SCAN staff member, who oversees the treatment plan and supervises the lay therapist assigned to the family. Regular staffings of each case are held twice a month with the lay therapist and monthly with Arkansas Social Services. The staff communicates with the lay therapist by phone, sometimes daily. A family is assigned to a lay therapist on the basis of the lay therapist's personal characteristics, experience, and skills in relation to the identified needs of the abusive family. The SCAN evaluator or other SCAN staff, who already established a relationship with the family, may introduce the family to the lay therapist.

Interface with State Agencies

Because in all states a state agency is mandated to provide child protective services, a program such as SCAN can only be effective when close coordination is ensured between the program and the mandated agency. Because SCAN is a Title XX contract funded by the social service agency, it is an integral part of the agency's program. Regular meetings are held with the executive director of SCAN and designated state agency personnel to negotiate contracts and funding, to provide information regarding fiscal and programmatic activities, and to discuss future directions of the program. SCAN also participates in program evaluations conducted by the state agency.

At the local level, cases are coordinated with social services in a formal manner by providing written and telephone reports regarding case management. This allows the state agency to carry out its mandate of monitoring protective service cases. Informally, SCAN staff and state agency staff communicate regarding cases as the need arises, which is often daily. Social services staff may also attend SCAN staffings.

Interface with Court System

SCAN works closely with the court system in each county to ensure that the legal process is followed and that both parents' and childrens' rights are appropriately considered. If for some reason the abusive parents are unwilling to cooperate with SCAN or if the children require foster care, social services is contacted, a petition is filed, and a court hearing is scheduled.

Parents are informed of their rights, and SCAN assists parents in receiving appropriate legal assistance. When a child is in foster care, SCAN requests a court review every three months.

Interface with Community Resources

SCAN interfaces with a number of community resources to provide community awareness of child abuse and child neglect. Resources are utilized during SCAN involvement, and parents are introduced to community resources as appropriate. Although initially in communities turf issues may be a problem, an informational approach by SCAN and success in initial cases overcomes resistance.

LAY THERAPISTS

SCAN recruits lay therapists through newspaper articles, radio, television, churches and civic groups. Most SCAN lay therapists are over thirty, are parents, are women, and have previous experiences in helping others. More and more SCAN lay therapists work, but this does not significantly effect recruitment or turnover of lay therapists. The best source of recruitment is other lay therapists in the SCAN program.

Training and Supervision

SCAN holds intensive two- to three-day training sessions for new lay therapists quarterly. The sessions are attended by usually forty-five or more individuals, including present lay therapists and staff. Sessions include the identification and dynamics of child abuse, the treatment approach, an overview of child and human development, and personal awareness exercises.

Following the training, the lay therapist is assigned to a family and receives supervision from the SCAN supervisor. Two weekly telephone contacts are made by the supervisor to oversee case management. Also, the lay therapist attends staffings twice monthly. Advanced training sessions are held at least quarterly at the local and state levels.

Prevention of Turnover

Most lay therapists remain with the SCAN program an average of eighteen to twenty-four months. Many leave to take jobs in social service programs, while some become employed by SCAN. Because the lay therapists are only paid fifty dollars per month for expenses and because abusive parents may be difficult to work with, the SCAN staff must provide positive support and supervision continuously.

The SCAN program is successful only if the lay therapist component is an integral part of the agency and the lay therapists are first priority. Lay therapists must be invited to feel a part of the agency and they must also have the knowledge, skill, and support in order to feel confident in working with the parents to whom they are assigned. Lay therapists remain in the SCAN program longer than other volunteer programs because they are performing significant functions in actually providing services to the families, rather than just babysitting or transportation.

SCAN AMERICA, INC.

SCAN America, Inc. opened in 1978 and entered into a three-party agreement between SCAN, the National Exchange Club Foundation for the Prevention of Child Abuse and Neglect, and the National Council of Juvenile and Family Court Judges. The National Exchange Club Foundation provided the funding.

SCAN America, Inc. successfully opened centers in the following states: North Carolina, Florida, Mississippi, Connecticut, Maryland, New Mexico, Texas, Tennessee, and Puerto Rico. These centers are in operation today.

The contract with the National Exchange Club Foundation for the Prevention of Child Abuse and Neglect ceased in April of 1983. SCAN America, Inc. plans to provide technical assistance to states in the future.

Chapter 9

SUMMARY

THE key element of the resocialization intervention model is the basic process of meeting developmental needs through socialization. This treatment emphasis provides an alternative model to the delivery of services for abusive parents. The advantage to this approach is that it serves to make available to parents an intensive and supportive ongoing relationship which is based upon helping parents meet their needs. Far more time is devoted in a consistent and supportive manner than is often available through many public welfare agencies, where caseloads range between thirty and fifty cases per worker. In many systems, social workers coordinate services performed by other agencies, rather than provide the actual services themselves.

Although the SCAN staff utilizes other resources within the community, the consistent relationship of a primary provider — a lay therapist — is always maintained. This is seen as a critical factor in the treatment process, since initially it may be expecting too much to begin directing abusive parents to a number of different agencies and individuals. The tremendous personal needs of abusive parents may be difficult to meet through services that are time limited. In addition, focus at the beginning of treatment on complex problem solving only serves to increase the parents' sense of anxiety and feelings of failure.

The SCAN program is successful in dealing with abusive parents because of several important factors. One is the extensive supportive network which SCAN provides, including well-trained volunteer lay therapists, who receive frequent in-service training and who are supervised on an intensive basis by program staff. In terms of training, which is specific to child abuse, the SCAN lay therapist and program staff is well ahead of employees in public protective service agencies.[1] Another factor contributing to the high level of service offered through SCAN lies in the qualities of their program staff and their lay therapists. SCAN utilizes the same qualities, from which it selects its program staff, to select its lay therapists which include:

(1) the ability to be empathetic, sincere, warm, accepting, mature and stable, and have a personal commitment toward helping parents;

(2) the ability to be mobile, a willingness to devote a maximum amount of time, positive attitudes about the potential of parents with an abuse problem, and positive parenting experiences as a child;

(3) a willingness to receive training in the dynamics of child abuse and human development;

(4) a comprehensive understanding of child development and an interest in the children;

(5) a positive self-concept and the ability to remain in an attachment relationship rather than a power position with another individual;

(6) the ability to express themselves in a gentle and supportive way, yet to be firm and consistent and to accept rebuff and rejection;

(7) the ability to nurture and respect the human worth of others.

The resocialization intervention model permeates the entire SCAN organization. All SCAN staff and lay therapists have a clear conceptualization of SCAN's overall mission and the intervention modality, as well as the characteristics of parents with whom they work.

Although SCAN is used throughout this book in describing the implementation of the resocialization approach, this framework can be adapted successfully by any family intervention program. A number of public social service agencies and mental health centers throughout the country, as well as other volunteer programs and private social service agencies, use various adaptations of this strategy of intervention. Additionally, any person involved in providing support to individual family members should find the concepts helpful.

Finally, it must be realized that no one specific approach to dealing with child maltreatment is a magic answer that works consistently well with each and every family. Much needs to be done in the areas of research and program evaluation to further delineate which approaches are most effective. However, from the perspective of many individuals who deal with abusive parents, the resocialization approach is one that is workable and achieves positive changes within families. The resocialization intervention approach is primarily a supportive network of individuals and agencies within a community that provides a humanitarian and behavioristic approach toward the reduction of child maltreatment among its community members.

EVALUATION OF THE SCAN PROGRAM

The SCAN program has been singled out for its success in dealing with abusive parents in several important areas. One is the extensive training provided for all new lay therapists, as well as the frequent in-service training. Other areas include the qualities of the lay therapists and the explicitly adhered to treatment philosophy followed in every SCAN case.

While little empirical data exists which clearly demonstrates the efficacy of this program, the SCAN program was evaluated in three communities over a three-year period as part of a national child abuse and neglect demonstration effort from 1974 through 1977. Berkeley Planning Associates conducted an evaluation of eleven projects throughout the country.[2] Their findings indicate that of all clients studied, those who are in treatment for six months or longer, and who also receive lay therapy or self-help group services such as Parents Anonymous, are most likely to show improvement in selected areas. These areas include the improvement of self-esteem, the development of more appropriate ways of expressing anger, the reduction of household stress situations, and the improvement of the ability to talk out problems.

The study suggests that programs such as SCAN may be more effective because they provide lay and group services, allow for more client contact, and more in-depth contact than others studied. The programs in the study which are determined to have the least success place an emphasis on the more traditional kinds of services. These strategies are normally associated with protective service agencies, which have large worker caseloads that inhibit the amount of time a worker can devote to any one client.[3]

In addition, the lay therapy model proved to be the least expensive of the different treatment models studied.[4] The cost of a lay therapy contract unit was $7.25, compared with a unit cost of $14.75 for individual counseling provided by professionals. The Berkeley Planning Associates study also found that the SCAN program reduced the use of foster care more significantly than other programs, both in terms of total number of children in care and length of time spent in foster care. The average stay in foster care for children placed through SCAN is six months; the national average is thirty-four months.

An additional assessment conducted by Community Research Application, Inc. for NIMH, in 1975 finds the SCAN program better able to provide services to difficult and demanding families than is possible through traditional public protective services. The small caseload (three per lay therapist at a maximum), the intensive commitment of the lay therapist to help families, and the sense of identity and motivation gained from being associated with a separate, autonomous entity, rather than being attached to some other organization, are highlighted as positive aspects of the SCAN program. This evaluation also emphasizes the purchase of service agreement between the public human services agency and SCAN, representing a private non-profit agency, and suggests the efficiency of allowing human service agencies to upgrade their community programs utilizing this approach. The SCAN program possesses considerable potential for additional research.

REPLICATION OF SCAN

SCAN moves slowly in developing additional centers to ensure that established programs maintain the quality of the initial SCAN effort. The program is viewed nationally as one which merits further attention. From 1978 to 1983, SCAN, the National Council of Juvenile and Family Court Judges, and the National Exchange Club developed a three-party agreement to implement the SCAN program in a number of sites nationally. The National Exchange Club Foundation for the Prevention of Child Abuse and Neglect provided funding and other support to achieve this goal in ten sites.

REFERENCES

1. Holmes, Monica, and Kagle, Arlene: *SCAN Volunteer Services, Inc.* New York, Community Research Application Inc., 1975, for the National Institute of Mental Health.
2. Berkeley Planning Associates: *Evaluation of the OCD-SRS National Demonstration Program on Child Abuse and Neglect.* Berkeley, 1977.
3. Ibid.
4. Ibid.
5. Child Welfare League of America: *Special Study,* 1982.
6. Holmes, Ibid.

Chapter 10

POSTSCRIPT

A FORMER ABUSIVE PARENT TALKS ABOUT
THE RESOCIALIZATION APPROACH

SHE brought me flowers: gardenias, camellias, different flowers. No one had ever brought me flowers. We live in an apartment, so I don't have a garden, and I love flowers. She did it because she's a caring person and that was how she expressed it. She was herself.

She let me talk. No one had ever really listened to me. She had time. She listened. She offered friendship with no strings. She didn't just say, "Remember your doctor's appointment Tuesday." She said, "I'll come by to pick you up on Tuesday." She let me depend on her.

To those people who say that dependence is no good, I disagree. I needed to be able to depend on someone else before I could depend on myself. You don't need to worry about people hanging on too long. Kids grow up when they're ready.

She didn't try to change *me*, but she set limits. She said the most caring things I had ever heard. She said, "I can't let you do that, but you can do all these other things, and we'll help you learn how." And she did, and she put me in touch with other people who did.

Later on, she helped me grow up. I was very low — I had just had a big disappointment — and I got hepatitis, along with several other members of my family. I was sure she would cancel her vacation, but she didn't. She said if I was going to die, I would have to wait till she got home. She modeled for me, and that was the turning point. I realized I would have to be good company for myself, and I began to take care of myself.

I have been asked what I wanted from my lay therapist. Well, here are some of the things I wanted....

I wanted her to show my husband what he was doing wrong — he wouldn't listen to me anymore.

I wanted her to see what an unruly and negative son I had — he was a monster.

I wanted her to know about my tragic childhood so that she would understand why I had turned out so badly.

I wanted her to listen to me whenever I felt like talking, and I wanted her to hear all the things I was not saying.

I wanted her to solve some of my most immediate problems: like, find a larger house with a fenced-in yard for us, figure out a way I could get a car of my own, and more money coming in. It would also help me feel better if she could tell my mother off for me, help me to find some friends I could relate to, sign me up for food stamps and Medicaid, call the bill collectors and explain that I needed time, find a dentist who would not charge to fix my teeth, and help my husband find a job with fewer working hours and a raise.

I wanted her to take the kids off my hands when I was down in the dumps and not make me feel guilty about not wanting them around all the time.

I wanted her to be the loving mother I never experienced and my perfect best friend.

I wanted her to like me all the time, not just when I was doing what she wanted me to; I wanted her to see something good in me, if there was anything good, and tell me about it; I wanted her to be real honest, unless it hurt.

I wanted her to take away some of the pain — I wanted her to fix me.

I wanted her to just love me: my way.

This, however, is what I got from my lay therapist....

I got a lay therapist who only wanted to hear about my husband from my husband.

I got no acknowledgement from her that my son was the monster I thought him to be. I did get plenty of information about typical behavior of children his age and a short course in child development and discipline. I also got permission from her not to like my children all the time.

I got to talk about my tragic childhood only when we had finished talking about the here and now, and we rarely ever got through with that.

I got a lay therapist who listened to me whenever I felt like talking, unless it infringed on her own personal or family time, and one who informed me that she did not possess ESP powers so what was left unsaid was also left unheard.

When it came to solving problems, my lay therapist didn't offer much. I learned to appreciate her predictability, "What have you thought of?" She offered suggestions and a few alternatives and left the rest up to me. (I did notice that she kept dropping hints about my going to work and all the advantages she could see in that.)

She helped me get day care and kindergarten for the kids. She was never my babysitter and let it be known quickly that that was not the reason she was on the scene. She assured me over and over again that it was okay not to want to be with my children twenty-four hours a day.

She did many things that a loving mother and a best friend would do, but she helped me to understand that she could never replace the mother I had missed, and for me to hold her up as the perfect best friend would be disastrous for us both.

She liked me all the time. All the time. No matter what I did or said she just kept right on liking me. "No wonder she's a lay therapist for SCAN with long hours, no pay or recognition," I often thought. "She's got a screw loose somewhere." No one in their right mind could keep on liking *me*.

She saw that something good in me that I wanted so much to be there. She told me how neat I was everytime we were together. I had trouble believing her in the beginning, but she persisted, and I decided she would not lie to me. I trusted her. She was real and she was honest and I could not deny that.

She did not take away my pain, but she encouraged me in a loving way to face it and deal with it when I was ready to. She was always there to make it less painful. She did not fix me. She showed me how I could fix me.

She loved me: her way.

This is what I learned....

I learned to solve problems.

I learned, for the most part, to let go of that ugly childhood.

I learned to have fun — not to chance, but by planning.

I learned to ask for what I want.

I learned to communicate.

I learned to feel potent, powerful, unique, and capable.

I learned to accept myself just as I am without demanding or even expecting perfection.

I learned to be nurturing to myself and others.

I learned to be aware of what I feel, hear, and see.

I learned to give up my children and my husband as mine — they belong to themselves.

I learned to love others without expecting that they do something for me in return — not always, but often.

I learned how important it is to give and receive strokes.

I learned how to feel free.

I got what I wanted — and so much more. It's called love.

Jackie Waddle
SCAN parent

APPENDICES

Appendix A

CHILD ABUSE AND NEGLECT REPORTING ACT

Ark. Statutes 42-807 - 42-818
(as amended)

42-807. Child Abuse and Neglect Reporting Act - Definitions.

(a) "Child" means any person under eighteen (18) years of age;

(b) "Abuse" means any physical injury, mental injury, sexual abuse, or sexual exploitation inflicted on a child other than by accidental means, or an injury which is at variance with the history given. The term encompasses both acts and omissions.

(c) "Neglect" means a failure to provide, by those legally responsible for the care and maintenance of the child the proper or necessary support; education, as required by law; or medical, surgical or any other care necessary for his well-being; or any maltreatment of the child. The term includes acts and omissions.

Provided, nothing in this Act (this section) shall be construed to imply that a child who is being furnished with treatment by spiritual means alone through a prayer, in accordance with the tenets and practices of a recognized church or religious denomination by a duly accredited practitioner thereof, is for this reason alone a neglected or dependent child within the meaning of this Act.

(d) "Sexual Abuse" includes rape and incest as defined in the Arkansas Criminal Code and Amendments thereto and any other offenses relating to sexual acts, abuse or exploitation as set out and defined in the Arkansas Criminal Code amendments thereto.

(e) "Sexual Exploitation" includes allowing, permitting, or encouraging a child to engage in prostitution by a person responsible for the child's welfare; and allowing, permitting, encouraging or engaging in the obscene photographing, filming, or depicting of a child for commercial purposes or for any use or purpose.

(f) "Unfounded Report" means any report made pursuant to this Act which is not supported by some credible evidence.

(g) "Department" means the County or State Social Services Division, Department of Human Services. (Acts 1975, No. 397, 2, p. 1057; 1979, No. 624, Sct. 1, p. 1279; 1981, No. 907, Sct. 1, p.)

42-808. REPORTS OF SUSPECTED ABUSE OR NEGLECT.

When any physician, surgeon, coroner, dentist, osteopath, resident, intern, registered nurse, hospital personnel (engaged in admission, examination, care or treatment of persons), teacher, school official, social service worker, day care center worker, or any other child or foster care worker, mental health professional, peace officer or law enforcement official has reasonable cause to suspect that a child has been subject to abuse, sexual abuse or neglect or observes the child being subject to conditions or circumstances which would reasonably result in abuse, he shall immediately report or cause a report to be made to the department. Whenever such person is required to report under this Act (Scts 42-807 - 42-818) in his capacity as a member of the staff of a medical or public or private institution, school, facility, or other agency, he shall immediately notify the person in charge of such institution, school, facility or other agency or his designated agent, who shall then become responsible for making a report or cause a report to be made.

In addition to those persons and officials required to report suspected child abuse, sexual abuse and/or neglect, any other person may make a report if such person has reasonable cause to suspect that a child has been abused or neglected. (Acts 1975, No. 397, Sct. 3, p. 1057.)

42.809. REPORTS OF DEATH CAUSED BY SUSPECTED ABUSE OR NEGLECT.

Any person or official required to report cases of suspected child abuse, sexual abuse or neglect, under Section 3 (Sct. 42-808) of this Act, including workers of the local child protective services, who has reasonable cause to suspect that a child has died as a result of child abuse, sexual abuse or neglect shall report that fact to the appropriate medical examiner or coroner. The medical examiner or coroner shall accept the report for investigation and shall report his findings to the police, the appropriate district attorney, the local child protective service agency and, if the institution making the report is a hospital, to the hospital. (Acts 1975, No. 397, Sct. 4, p. 1057.)

42.810. PHOTOGRAPHS AND X-RAYS.

Any person who is required to report cases of child abuse, sexual abuse and/or neglect may take or cause to be taken, at public expense, color photographs of the areas of trauma visible on a child and, if medically indicated, cause to be performed radiological examinations of the child. Any photographs and/or x-rays taken shall be sent to the department as soon as possible. Whenever such person is required to report under this Act. (Sct. 42-807 - 42-818), in his capacity as a member of the staff of a medical or other private or public institution, school, facility or agency, he shall immediately notify the person in charge of such institution, school, facility or agency or his designated delegate, who shall then take or cause to be taken, at public expense, color photographs of physical trauma and shall, if medically indicated, cause to be performed radiological examination of the child. (Acts 1975, No. 397, Sct. 5, p. 1057.)

42.811. PROTECTIVE CUSTODY OF CHILDREN.

A police officer, a law enforcement official or a designated employee of the city or county department of social services, may take a child into protective custody or any person in charge of a hospital or similar institution or any physician treating a child may keep that child in his custody without the consent of the parent or the guardian, whether or not additional medical treatment is required if the circumstances or conditions of the child are such that continuing in his place of residence or in the care and custody of the parent, guardian, custodian or other person responsible for the child's care presents an imminent danger to that child's life or health; provided, however, that such custody does not exceed seventy-two (72) hours and that the juvenile court and the department are notified immediately in order that child-protective proceedings may be initiated. The director of the local social services or health agency may give effective consent for medical, dental, health and hospital services for any abused child under the age of eighteen (18) years. (Acts 1975, No. 397, Sct. 6, p. 1057.)

42.812. REPORTS — TIME TO BE MADE — CONTENTS — AVAILABILITY TO LAW ENFORCEMENT AGENCY — EVIDENCE.

(a) Reports of child abuse, sexual abuse and neglect made pursuant to this Act (Scts 42-807 - 42-818) shall be made immediately by telephone and shall be followed by a written report within forty-eight hours if so requested by the receiving agency. The receiving agency shall immediately forward a copy of this report to the statewide central registry on forms supplied by said registry.

(b) Such reports shall include the following information: the names and address of the child and his parents or other persons responsible for his care, if known; the child's age, sex, and race; the nature and extent of the child's injuries, sexual abuse or neglect, including any evidence of previous injuries, sexual abuse or neglect, to the child or his siblings; the name and address of the person responsible for the injuries, sexual abuse or neglect, if known; family composition; the source of the report, the person making the report, his occupation and where he can be reached; the actions taken by the reporting source, including the taking of photographs and x-rays, removal or keeping of the child or notifying the coroner, medical examiner and other information that the person making the report believes may be helpful in the furtherance of the purposes of this Act.

(c) A copy of this report shall immediately be made available to the local prosecuting attorney's office for consideration.

(d) A written report from persons or officials required by the Act to report shall be admissible in evidence in any proceeding relating to child abuse, sexual abuse or neglect. (Acts 1975, No. 397, Sct. 7, p. 1057.)

42.813. INVESTIGATION OF REPORTS — EXAMINATIONS OF CHILDREN.

(a) The department shall make a thorough investigation promptly upon receiving either the oral or the written report. The primary purpose of such an investigation shall be the protection of the child.

(b) The investigation shall include the nature, extent and cause of the child abuse, sexual abuse or neglect; the identity of the person responsible therefore; the names and conditions of other children in the home; and evaluation of the parents or persons responsible for the care of the child; the home environment and the relationship of the child(ren) to the parents or other persons responsible for their care; and all other pertinent data.

(c) The investigation shall include a visit to the child's home, a physical, psychological or psychiatric examination of all children in that home, and an interview with the subject child. If the admission to the home, school or any other place that the child may be, or permission of the parent or other persons responsible for the child(ren) for the physical, psychological or psychiatric examination cannot be obtained, then the juvenile court or the district court, upon cause shown, shall order the parents or persons responsible and in charge of any place where the child may be to allow entrance for the interview, above examinations and investigations.

(d) If, before the examination is complete, the opinion of the investigators is that immediate removal is necessary to protect the child(ren) from further abuse or neglect, the juvenile court or the district court, on petition by the investigators and with good cause being shown, shall issue an order for temporary removal and custody.

(e) The county agency responsible for the protection of juveniles or county welfare unit, shall make a complete written report of the investigation together with its recommendations. Such reports shall be made available to the juvenile court or district court, the district attorney and the appropriate law enforcement agency upon request.

(f) The department shall make a written report or case summary, together with services offered and accepted, to the state central registry on forms supplied by the registry for that purpose. (Acts 1975, No. 397, Sct. 8, p: 1057.)

(g) When an employee or agent of the department is reported as being suspected of child abuse, neglect or exploitation, the prosecuting attorney or local law enforcement official will conduct the investigation. (Acts 1975, No. 397, Sct. 8, p. 1057; 1979, No. 624, Sct. 3, p. 1279.)

42.814. GOOD FAITH REPORT—IMMUNITY FROM LIABILITY.

Any person, official or institution participating in good faith in the making of a report, the taking of photographs or the removal of a child pursuant to this ACT (Scts. 42-807 - 42-818), shall have immunity from any liability, civil or criminal, that otherwise might result by reason of such actions. For the purpose of any proceedings, civil or criminal, the good faith of any person required to report cases of child abuse, sexual abuse or neglect shall be presumed. (Acts 1975, No. 397, Sct. 9, p. 1057.)

42-815. PRIVILEGED COMMUNICATION NOT GROUNDS FOR EXCLUDING EVIDENCE — EXCEPTION.

Any provision of the Arkansas Uniform Rules of Evidence (Act 1143 of 1975, 1976 Extended Session, Sct. 28-1001) notwithstanding, any privilege between husband and wife or between any professional person, except lawyer and client, including but not limited to physicians, ministers, counselors, hospitals, clinics, day care centers, and schools and their clients, shall not constitute grounds for excluding evidence at any proceeding regarding child abuse, sexual abuse, or neglect of a child or the cause thereof. (Acts 1975, No. 397, 10, p. 1057; 1979, No. 75, Sct. 1, p. 162.)

42.816. PENALTY FOR VIOLATIONS — CIVIL LIABILITY.

(a) Any person, official or institution required by this Act (Scts. 42-807 - 42-818) to report a case of suspected child abuse, sexual abuse or neglect, who willfully fails to do so shall be subject to a fine of one hundred dollars ($100) and up to five (5) days in jail.

(b) Any person, official or institution required by this Act to report a case of suspected child abuse, sexual abuse, or neglect, and who willfully fails to do so, shall be civilly liable (for damages) proximately caused by such failure. (Acts 1975, No. 397, Sct. 11, p. 1057.)

42-817. GUARDIAN AD LITEM APPOINTED — EXAMINATIONS OF PARENTS.

(a) The Court, in every case filed under this Act (Scts. 42-807 - 42-818), shall appoint a guardian ad litem for the child. The guardian shall be given access to all reports relevant to the case and to any reports of examination of the child's parents or other custodian pursuant to this Act. The guardian ad litem shall, in general, be charged with the representation of the child's best interests. To that end, he shall make such further investigation that he deems necessary to ascertain the facts, to interview witnesses, examine and cross-examine witnesses in both the adjudicatory and dispositional hearings, make recommendations to the court and participate further in the proceedings to the degree appropriate for adequately representing the child.

(b) At any time after the completion of the adjudicatory hearing of a case of child abuse, sexual abuse or neglect and a finding of dependency therein, the court may, on its own motion, or the motion of the guardian ad litem, order the examination by the physician, psychologist or psychiatrist, of any parent or other person having custody of the child at the time of the alleged abuse, sexual abuse or neglect, if the court finds such an examination is necessary to the proper determination of the dispositional hearing of the case. The dispositional hearing may be continued pending the completion of such examination. The physician, psychologist or psychiatrist conducting such an examination may be required to testify in the dispositional hearing concerning the results of such examination and may be asked to give his opinion as to whether the protection of the child requires that he not be returned to the custody of his parents or other persons having custody of him at the time of the alleged abuse, sexual abuse or neglect. The rules of evidence as provided by law shall apply to such testimony except that the physician, psychologist or psychiatrist shall be allowed to testify to conclusions reached from the hospital, medical, psychological or laboratory records, tests, or reports, provided the same are produced at the hearing. Persons so testifying shall be subject to cross-examination as are other witnesses. No evidence acquired as a result of any such examination of the parent or any other person having custody of the child may be used against such in any subsequent criminal proceeding against such person or custodian concerning the abuse or nonaccidental injury of the child. (Acts 1975, No. 397, Sct. 12, p. 1057.)

42-818.　STATEWIDE CENTRAL REGISTRY—RECORDS—RELEASE OF INFORMATION—AMENDMENT OR EXPUNGEMENT—PENALTY.

(a) (1) There shall be established within the Family Service Division of the State Welfare Department (Division of Social Services), a statewide central registry for child abuse, sexual abuse and neglect made pursuant to this Act. (Scts. 42-807 - 42-818.)

(2) There shall be a single statewide telephone number that all persons whether mandated by law or not, may use to report cases of suspected child abuse, sexual abuse and neglect and that all persons so authorized by this Act may use for determining the existence of

prior records in order to evaluate the condition or circumstances of the child before them. Such oral telephone reports shall immediately be transmitted by the central registry to the local child protective services. If the records indicate a previous report concerning the subject of the report or other pertinent information, the appropriate local protective agency shall be notified of these facts.

(3) The central registry shall contain, but shall not be limited to: all information in the written report; record of the final disposition of the report including services offered and services accepted; the plan for rehabilitative treatment; the names and identifying data, dates and circumstances of any persons requesting or receiving information from the registry; and any other information which might be helpful in furthering the purposes of this Act.

(4) Reports made pursuant to the Act, as well as any other information obtained, and reports written or photographs taken concerning such reports in the possession of the department (division) shall be confidential and shall be made available to: (a) a physician who has before him a child whom he reasonably believes may have been abused, sexually abused or neglected; (b) a person authorized to place a child in protective custody when such person has before him a child whom he reasonably believes may have been abused, sexually abused and/or neglected and such person requires such information to determine whether to place such child in protective custody; (c) a duly authorized agency having responsibility for the care or supervision of the subject of a report; (d) any person who is the subject of a report; (e) a court where it determines that such information is necessary for the determination of an issue before the court; (f) appropriate state or local officials responsible for administration, supervision or legislation in relation to the prevention or treatment of child abuse or neglect when carrying out their official functions and (g) any person engaged in bona fide research or audit purposes, provided however, that no information identifying the subjects of the report shall be made available to the researcher unless it is absolutely essential to the research purpose, suitable provision is made to maintain confidentiality of the data, and the commissioner of the department gives prior written approval. The commissioner shall establish by regulation, criteria for the application of this subsection.

After a child, who is the subject of a report, reaches the age of eighteen (18) years, access to a child's record under subsections A and B of this section shall be permitted only if a sibling or offspring of such child is before such person and is a suspected victim of child abuse, sexual abuse and/or neglect. In addition, a physician or person in charge of an institution or agency making a report shall receive, upon request, a summary of the findings and action taken by the local child protection agency in response to the report. The amount of such detail shall depend upon the sources of the report and shall be established by regulations created by the commissioner of the central registry. However, under no circumstances shall the information be released unless the person's or official's capacity is confirmed by the department (division) and the released information states whether or not the report is founded or unfounded. A person given access to the names or other information identifying a subject of the report, except the subject of the report, shall not divulge or make public such identifying information unless he is the district attorney or other law enforcement official and the purpose is to initiate court action.

(5) Unless an investigation of a report conducted pursuant to this Act determines there is some credible evidence of alleged abuse, sexual abuse or neglect, all information identifying on the subject of the report shall be expunged from the central registry forthwith.

(6) In all other cases, the record of the report to the central registry shall be sealed at no later than ten (10) years after the subject child's eighteenth (18th) birthday. Once sealed, the record shall not otherwise be available, unless the commissioner of the central registry upon notice to the subjects of the report, gives his personal approval for an appropriate reason. In any case, and at any time, the commissioner may amend, seal or expunge any record upon good cause shown and notice to the subjects of the report.

(7) At any time, the subject of a report may receive, upon request, a report of all information contained in the central registry; provided, however, that the commissioner is authorized to prohibit the release of data that would identify the person who made the report or who cooperated in subsequent investigation which he reasonably finds to be detrimental to the safety or interests of such person.

(8) At any time, subsequent to the competion (completion) of the investigation, but in no event later than ninety (90) days after the receipt of a report, a subject of the report may request the commissioner to amend, seal or expunge the record of the report. If the commissioner refuses or does not act within a reasonable time, but in no event later than thirty (30) days after such a request, the subject shall have the right to a fair hearing to determine whether the record of the report in the central registry should be amended or expunged on the grounds that it is inaccurate or it is being maintained in a manner inconsistent with this Act. The appropriate local child protective agency shall be given fair notice of the hearing. The burden, in such a hearing, shall be on the department (division) and the appropriate local child protective services. In such hearings, the fact that there was such a finding of child abuse, sexual abuse or neglect shall be presumptive evidence that the report was substantiated.

(9) Written notice of any amendment or expungement made pursuant to the provisions of this Act, shall be served on each subject of such report and to the appropriate local child protective service. The latter, upon receipt of such notice, shall take similar action regarding any central local registry for child abuse, sexual abuse, and/or neglect.

(10) Any person who willfully permits and any other person who encourages the release of data or information contained in the central registry to persons not permitted by this Act, shall be guilty of a Class A misdemeanor.

(B) The central registry may adopt such rules and regulations as may be necessary to encourage cooperation with other states in exchanging reports to effect a national registration system. (Acts 1975, No. 397, Sct. 13, p. 1057.)

Appendix B

WHY DO WE USE THE COURT?

IN many families, SCAN can leave children in the home and work with a family on a voluntary basis still insuring safety for the child.

If an investigation is substantiated and SCAN opens a case, a court hearing may be necessary for the following reasons.

1. There is evidence to support the belief that the child(ren) may be in danger of further abuse if left in the home.
2. The family is uncooperative and SCAN cannot visit the home on a voluntary basis.
3. The age and severity of abuse are such that the child's(ren's) life and health are in jeopardy.
4. Even though SCAN may wish to leave the child(ren) in the home, the parents benefit from hearing the information about the abuse in a formal setting and receiving specific direction from the court.

Remember, holding a court hearing and stating to the parents that they are responsible for the safety of their child(ren) is difficult and painful for everyone, but the court can be used as a therapeutic tool and will not ruin a relationship with the parents. It is important that the truth is stated openly, and SCAN provides support and aid for the parents throughout the hearing and after.

Appendix C

THE DECISION-MAKING PROCESS

1. If you believe that foster care is necessary, contact your state coordinator or designated supervisor. Give all facts, including the original report and immediate problems, and any documentation of abuse that you have (hospital, physician, etc.). Be able to present any possible alternatives to foster care placement, such as relatives, etc.
2. If you and your supervisor agree that foster care is needed, call your local social services representative and give the same information, and if it appears necessary, request a joint staffing to make the final decision.
3. If you and the social services agree to foster care, prepare a petition in conjunction with the social services or SCAN attorney. (In some counties, SCAN fills out the petition; in others, social services gets the petition completed, and the SCAN director co-signs.) When you give information for the petition, give facts, information which you personally know, or facts which have been identified by a creditable source (e.g. medical doctor, school nurse). Never use hearsay evidence, such as "The neighbor says" or "The whole school knows...." The petition must be signed and notarized. In some counties, SCAN and social services co-sign the petition.
4. If there has been a medical examination of the injuries, get a "battered child" report from the doctor, hospital, or medical person who saw the child. Definition of a petition: A petition is a request for the juvenile court to hear a complaint involving the welfare of a child. No court action can be initiated without a peti-

tion, even if parents request that their child be placed in foster care. A parent may voluntarily place their child(ren) in foster care by signing a special form. The style of form and the decision on whether or not the parents are required to appear in court may vary from county to county. It is important to establish a procedure with your local social services representative and juvenile judge as soon as possible.

5. Social services or the designated attorney will request a court date and a time of hearing, unless this has been otherwise delegated to SCAN. If SCAN requests a time, it must be cleared with social services and the SCAN attorney or social services attorney.

6. A summons to court will be sent to the parents (or guardian) of the child, along with a copy of the petition to inform them of the hearing with a copy of the petition to inform them of the allegations and the facts to be heard. Always personally inform both parents and witnesses prior to service of the summons.

   A subpoena is sent to any witnesses who are expected to testify at the hearing. Do not forget to subpoena any medical records concerning the case if a medical person will testify. Both summons and a subpoena are legal documents and will be delivered or telephoned by the juvenile court or the county sheriff's department.

Appendix D

CRITERIA FOR CONSIDERING
FOSTER CARE

1. Age of the child
2. The extent of injuries/extent of child abuse dynamics
3. Ability of parents to maintain control
4. Willingness of parents to cooperate
5. Available resources in the community, such as day care, mental health, etc.
6. Family members who offer support system, bail out
7. Substance abuse
8. Repeated abuse after SCAN enters home
9. Ability of parents to learn new methods of discipline
10. Emotional condition of child
11. Emotional condition of parents
12. Degree of isolation of family
13. Stress level—home

All of the abuse factors would be examined if foster care is considered. Your decision must be made according to the situation of each individual family as it corresponds with the abuse conditions.

Appendix E

LEGAL DOCUMENTS

A. Petition

A PETITION presents a formal request to the court to hear the facts of why a child should be found "dependent and neglected" and protected from further harm.

A petition will be:

1. Prepared by the SCAN or social services local office, or the SCAN or social services attorney.
2. Signed by the county director and may or may not be co-signed by the social services county director.
3. Filed with the county clerk after the signatures have been notarized.
4. Accompanied by a concise, short statement of the facts of abuse that can be proven by testimony (medical, SCAN or other professional personnel).
5. Filed before *any* court action can be initiated, even if parents are willing to place child(ren) in custody voluntarily.
6. In a legal form acceptable to the local judge or referee. A copy of the petition will be presented to:
   a. Local county clerk
   b. Parents and parents' attorney
   c. Local juvenile court (if separate from county clerk)
   d. Local social services office
   e. Local social services and/or SCAN attorney
   f. SCAN file

It is important not to include as facts any hearsay reports. Only include facts that can be proved by your own knowledge or medical or expert testimony.

B. Summons

Parents or legal guardians of the child(ren) will be served (by the sheriff's department or juvenile court) a copy of the petition and a legal summons to attend court. The summons notifies the parents of the time and place of the court hearing, the advisability of securing an attorney, and the facts of the allegations concerning the child.

C. Subpoena

Subpoenas are legal documents issued to witnesses requiring their presence at the court hearing. The subpoenas notify the witness of the time and place of the hearing and the fact that a warrant can be issued for nonappearance.

A subpoena should be issued to *all* witnesses for their protection and to insure that all records appropriate to the child(ren) are also available to the court. In order to insure that medical and other confidential records are subpoenaed, identify the "keeper of the records" in the subpoena, and subpoena these records separately.

It is important to be certain that all legal parents or guardians are notified of any court action concerning a child. If one parent's whereabouts is unknown, legal requirements are satisfied by publishing for 20 days a newspaper request for that person to respond to the appropriate court.

1. A petition must be filed to request a hearing.
2. A petition should have correct facts that can be testified to by credible witnesses.
3. Make sure social services has all facts about the case and the attorney has appropriate information.
4. Summons are sent to all legal parents or guardians with proper address.
5. Subpoenas are sent to all witnesses, and appropriate records are also subpoenaed with "keeper of records."
6. Parents and witnesses are contacted before the hearing about the facts of the case and their testimony.

D. Court Orders

A court order is the written statement of the judge's decision. If the judge concurs with SCAN's recommendations, they will be included in the order of stipulations.

The SCAN or social services attorney is usually responsible for preparing the order for the judge's signature.

An order is not legal without the judge's signature and must be filed with the county clerk. Social services local office and the attorneys will receive a copy of the order as well as the juvenile court and SCAN.

An emergency order may be obtained from the juvenile judge or referee by giving "probable cause" testimony to the judge and requesting an order for immediate custody. The local law enforcement agency will be ordered to aid in picking up the child(ren) and transporting them to the hospital or social services foster worker.

Appendix F

HOW TO PREPARE A COURT SUMMARY

1. Review with your staff or the lay therapist and state coordinator all of the information that you have.
2. Write a concise but complete summary of the facts in the case for the court. State the original referral and give significant information concerning abuse incidents, dynamics of abuse, etc. Be sure to include any medical documentation. Include both positive and negative aspects of the case. Include your recommendations, such as foster care, relative, etc. Include the stipulations the family must meet before their child will be returned to the home. Ask that the stipulations be included in orders by court. Give a copy of the summary to your social service representative and attorney before the hearing. Be familiar with testimony of all your witnesses. Answer questions directly and specifically. Do not be defensive.

Appendix G

COURT SUMMARY

A CONCISE summary of SCAN involvement with the family (1-1½ pages) containing:
1. History of work with parents (time span, number of contacts, dynamics)
2. History of child(ren) (foster care, past and current injuries, information from other agencies)
3. Family involvement with other agencies
4. Written reports (battered child report, mental health)
5. Lack of progress as well as positive progress

Appendix H

TYPES OF HEARINGS

A. Emergency Hearing and Order

IF SCAN has information that there is "probable cause" to believe that a child's(ren's) health or safety is in danger, a petition is prepared and the judge is asked for an emergency order.

Be certain there is sufficient evidence that a child may be in immediate danger. Take into consideration the:

1. Child's age
2. Severity of injury
3. General physical condition
4. Past history of abuse or neglect

If an emergency order is issued for "probable cause," a hearing date for an adjudicatory hearing is set. The parents have a right to have this hearing within 72 hours, or their attorney can request the hearing be postponed. If this occurs, the child will remain in custody until the hearing. Be sure to advise the parents to secure an attorney.

B. The Adjudicatory Hearing

The "burden of proof" is on SCAN if a petition is filed with allegations of abuse and neglect. A "preponderance of evidence" is necessary to win a case in an adversary hearing (parents contesting the child's removal). The adjudicatory hearing must be decided in SCAN's favor for a child to remain in foster care or a court order to remain in effect. Proof "beyond a reasonable doubt" is necessary only for criminal prosecution.

Remember, prepare a case as if you were going against the best attorney in the country.

1. Prepare witnesses and have professionals if possible (doctor, nurse, social worker).
2. Be sure legal documents are prepared correctly.
3. Be sure parents are summoned.
4. Be sure witnesses are subpoenaed.
5. Have *all* records available.
6. Use expert witnesses if possible.

C. Review Hearing

If possible, set up a regular review of the case in a specific time frame (30 days, 90 days) when the adjudication hearing is over.

Reviews are important to remind both the agency and the client of their obligation to the court and the child.

Regular reviews will also insure that the child does not "get lost" in the foster care system. SCAN will attempt to return a child to his/her home if the child can be safe and receive positive parenting.

D. Supervisory Hearing

In some juvenile court hearings, SCAN and social services do not wish to remove the child(ren) from the home but do need the structure of court orders to work in the home.

In this type of hearing, legal custody of the child(ren) will be given to Arkansas Social Services to insure the continued involvement of SCAN in the home, but physical custody will remain with the parents.

If a child continues to be abused after a supervisory hearing, it will be necessary to request a hearing or order for removal of the child from the home to foster care.

Appendix I
GUARDIAN (OR ATTORNEY) AD LITEM

A CT 397 stipulates that a guardian ad litem will be appointed by the court for every child involved in an abuse/neglect hearing. Some counties have no money to implement this order.

The guardian is to represent only the best interests of the child. SCAN and the guardian can share information and coordinate services to the family. It is best to coordinate on the front end, and be sure the guardian is aware of SCAN's goals and activities.

Appendix J

PREPARING THE CASE

A. *How Will We Prove Our Facts?*

1. By presenting competent reliable evidence such as medical personnel, mental health professionals, eyewitness or "with our knowledge" accounts of what happened by the evaluator or other witnesses.

2. Hearsay evidence is incompetent evidence, or secondhand knowledge, and cannot be verified by the credibility of the out-of-court witness.

   Example: 1. Written documents whose author is not in court.

   2. A witness stating what someone else said or saw.

   3. A witness relating conclusions rather than stating facts, such as "I knew he was furious" instead of "I saw him beat on the door, slap the child, and hit his wife."

3. Case records. Official records kept in the course of business and entered into evidence by the "keeper of the records."

   Example: Medical records; SCAN records of contacts with a family are exceptions to the hearsay rule.

4. Photographs of a child may be taken (see Act 397) by the investigating agency, and also by the hospital in the course of investigation or by a law enforcement agency. The reality of seeing the injuries in court is helpful in presenting a case.

5. Depositions are taken from a witness prior to a hearing when a witness cannot be in court. A deposition is a typed certified transcript of the witness' testimony with both attorneys and a court reporter present. It is expensive and rarely done.

6. Interrogatories are taken when a witness is not available for the hearing. The opposing attorneys each present a list of questions; the court reporter asks and transcribes answers to the questions. This record is certified and presented at the hearing.

7. Expert witnesses are professionals (physicians, psychologists, psychiatrists, social workers, etc.) who are qualified in the court as persons able to present an opinion concerning a condition or another person. If an "expert" is part of a case presentation, make sure he/she can present credentials if the opposing attorney chooses to "voir dire" (question) the witness' expert qualifications.

8. History and recommendations about the family from SCAN aid the court in a "way to go" to help the family.

B. Preparing a Witness

1. Be aware of the exact information a witness can testify to so that your attorney can ask specific questions. Give him a list of those questions if possible.

2. Remind the witness:
   a. Of the proper mode of dress in court;
   b. To answer truthfully;
   c. To say "I don't know" if they don't know;
   d. Not to become angry or defensive when questioned, but to remain calm and give short, concise answers;
   e. To be on time; and
   f. To be respectful of the court.

3. Go over the testimony you expect from a witness and see if dates and times agree.

4. Assemble correspondence, professional evaluations, and documentation of visits in chronological order. You may use notes or case records to assist your memory on the witness stand.

C. *How to Testify*

1. Remember, you are a valuable witness because you know the facts in this case better than anyone else in the court-room.
2. You have a carefully documented case record. Be organized.
3. Think about answers; tell positives as well as negatives in the home.

D. *Recommendations*

During SCAN and social services staffings write down specific logical recommendations to help the family. (Example: A physical exam for the child every two weeks. Mr. and Mrs. B. will receive a psychological evaluation at the mental health center.)

Written recommendations should accompany each court summary and may be included in the court order as stipulations for the family to follow in order to insure the child's safety in, or return to, the home.

If a court case is prepared carefully, using the court case checklist, to jog memory you will have:

1. A petition that has been filed and facts stated.
2. Arkansas Social Services and state office input and knowledge of hearing.
3. Family summonsed and personally contacted.
4. Witnesses subpoenaed.
5. Witnesses testimony specified and questions prepared for each witness. Individual preparation is necessary.
6. Prepared summary of history and recommendations for the court.

Appendix K

APPEALS AND GUARDIANSHIP

A. *Appeal*

IF a client or agency is not satisfied with a juvenile court decision, the client's or agency's attorney may appeal that decision to the circuit court of appeals.

At that time, the evidence given in juvenile court is reheard by the circuit judge. A decision is handed down to reverse the juvenile court decision or to return the case to juvenile court and uphold their decision.

B. *Guardianship*

When a child has been placed in foster care, and SCAN has worked with a family for six months or more, it is advisable to work out a plan to return a child to the home. If SCAN can provide support and supervision in the home and SCAN believes the child will be safe in the parent's home, Arkansas Social Services and SCAN will make a decision on this recommendation prior to a court hearing.

At this time, there is documentation of and court review of:
1. Parent and child visits
2. Cooperation of parents with SCAN and other agencies
3. Intervention of other agencies and support in the home
4. Child's(ren's) needs — current and future.

There must be an early decision in the case to request custody of the child, or to request supervision in the home while the child stays there.

Be prepared to provide facts why one or the other is the best plan. Keep in mind:

1. The age of the child
2. Severity of abuse
3. Cooperation (or lack of) by parents
4. SCAN ability to support and monitor the home
5. Parent's problems and future needs

If it is determined that the child(ren) will not be safe with their parents, SCAN and social services will recommend that the juvenile court grant permanent custody to Arkansas Social Services who may then proceed for guardianship in chancery court.

After recommending guardianship, SCAN will no longer be involved in visitation or treatment with the family unless continuing to protect another child in that family.

Appendix L

GUARDIANSHIP NARRATIVE SUMMARY

THIS should include:
1. Brief background summary including a physical description of the child's developmental and medical information.
2. Dated chronological summary of contacts with the family; their involvement in any plans made for the children; the fact that the parents have been informed of the division's plans to file for guardianship, etc.
3. Reason for requesting guardianship.
4. Date of parents' marriage and/or divorce, if applicable.
5. Any other pertinent information that should be helpful in making a decision on the case.
   a. Last known address of both parents (not a post office box number).
   b. Full legal name of child's mother, including her maiden name.
   c. Full legal name of the child's legal father or of putative father if he is named on the juvenile court order or birth certificate, has acknowledged paternity, or has assumed any responsibility for the child.

Appendix M

SCAN RESPONSIBILITIES DURING FOSTER CARE PERIOD

S CAN will continue to work with the parent(s) to help them regain custody of their child(ren), if possible.

One of the primary responsibilities is to help transport, arrange and supervise foster care visits between parent(s) and child(ren).

SCAN will:

1. Coordinate with Arkansas Social Services to arrange visits at a convenient time for parents, foster parents and child. We will attempt to give Arkansas Social Services 3-7 days notice for all visits. (Actual time will depend on the agreement between individual SCAN and social services local offices.)

2. Transport parent(s) and child(ren) for at least 50 percent of the transportation needs. Lay therapists, staff and transportation volunteers may be used here.

3. Visits begin in the SCAN or social services office for approximately one to two hours and are supervised by the lay therapist or staff (see visit description in forms). Longer supervised visits may be held at the office or family home if early visits are successful and the lay therapist and staff are content with the parent's and children's behavior.

After treatment in the family has continued and visits have been successful, day and weekend visits with "drop-in" supervision by the lay therapist may begin.

Information on foster care visits should be given to Arkansas

Social Services during staffings of the joint case and in writing for their records. The written records may be in a form or as minutes taken at the joint staffing.

SCAN must also advise the court of the progress of the visits during a review and in a written court summary. A written record of the lack of visits, missed visits, poor interaction between parent and child, and the uncooperative stance of a family may be used as evidence for the necessity of guardianship.

Good progress in treatment and visits where parents use new skills and information to play and discipline children also are valuable to the court.

    4. To insure adherence to Title XX regulations and the State Administrative Review Committee (S.A.R.C.) guidelines, SCAN will include a written report of foster care visits held in the SCAN office for local social services files. SCAN will also provide the local social services office with copies of all summaries, mental health evaluations, court documents and significant correspondence concerning a family when the family is a joint case of SCAN and social services (foster care of supervisory custody).

Appendix N

COURT AND AGENCY PREPARATION
FOR RETURN OF CHILD FROM
FOSTER CARE

THE goal of both social services and SCAN in utilizing foster care as a temporary placement for child(ren) unable to live at home is to return the child(ren) to a safe, stable home.

During the treatment process, regular reviews should have proceeded with the local social services office on a monthly basis, and the juvenile court on a 90-day basis or more frequently.

Once the county director, state coordinator and social services coordinator are in agreement, the plan for return of the child should be presented to the SCAN and/or social services attorney.

The plan should include:

1. The summary of the court, including:
   a. progress in specific areas
   b. lack of progress in specific areas
   c. attitude of the parents
   d. history of visitation, both frequency and interaction
   e. specific recommendations to the court concerning how SCAN will monitor and support the home after the child is returned from foster care.

If a regular review is not scheduled, SCAN or social services attorney shall contact the juvenile court to request a court hearing considering return of the child.

In some counties, a new petition setting forth your request must be filed. In other counties, the original petition is considered the only one necessary.

When it is resolved that the decision is to ask for return of the child(ren) to the home:

1. Meet with the family.
2. Include the lay therapist in all plans for change in the home.
3. Remind the family that the court will make the final decision in any change of custody.
4. Encourage the family to secure an attorney if they have any reservation about the safeguards SCAN is requesting from the court in order for their child to be returned.

INDEX